W O R K S

The Architecture of

A.J. Diamond, Donald Schmitt

and Company, 1968 – 1995

Documents in Canadian Architecture

WORKS: The Architecture of A.J. Diamond, Donald Schmitt and Company, 1968 – 1995

TUNS Press
Faculty of Architecture
Technical University of Nova Scotia
P.O. Box 1000
Halifax, Nova Scotia
Canada B3J 2X4

Director: Frank Palermo
General Editor: Esmail Baniassad
Manager: Donald Westin

Editor: Brian Carter
Design: Bhandari & Co.
Co-ordination: Steven Evans
Editing: Ruth Crow
Research assistant: Heather Lyons
Bibliographic research: Dale Moore
Production: Donald Westin
Film Separations: Atlantic Nova Print Co. Inc.
Printing: Atlantic Nova Print Co. Inc.

Canadian Cataloguing in Publication Data
Main entry under title:
WORKS: The Architecture of A.J. Diamond, Donald Schmitt and Company, 1968 – 1995

     (Documents in Canadian Architecture)
     ISBN 0-929112-31-8

1. A.J. Diamond, Donald Schmitt and Company. 2. Architecture, Modern – 20th century – Ontario – Designs and plans. I. Carter, Brian. II. A.J. Diamond, Donald Schmitt and Company. III. Series.

NA749.A53A4 1995   720.92'271   C95-950077-4

TABLE OF CONTENTS

FOREWORD

BY ESMAIL BANIASSAD

This book is about the work of A.J. Diamond, Donald Schmitt and Company, a firm which has made a consistently valuable contribution to the search for an architecture of the public domain. Their work demonstrates that buildings can succeed both as individual works of architecture and as part of an aggregate contributing to the collective good – each complete in itself and as complementary elements of the city. In both respects the new City Hall in Jerusalem provides a good example.

There is a point on the plaza in front of the new City Hall from which you can see the wall of the Old City, the domes of the Armenian churches, and the beginning of the City Hall complex. Here the 16th century wall of the Ottoman Empire is as much part of the physical context as is the 20th century office building by Mendelsohn. In many ways this typifies the work of A.J. Diamond, Donald Schmitt and Company.

In Jerusalem one does not have to recall history – it asserts itself. It forms a context within which the influence of the City on art and literature become manifest. Here the material and the metaphysical become one. The past and the future exist in an eternal present. The fabric of the Old City is woven with strands from the Judeo-Christian emphasis on spirituality and the Hellenistic celebration of the body. This is the context which consciously or subconsciously seems to permeate much of the firm's work. It is a context of sensitivity to existing buildings, awareness of new conditions, skillful handling of design as craft rather than preoccupation with style.

Beyond the requisite conditions of human accommodation, architects must at best embody an expression of the public institution. The challenge this poses is that such expression must be a celebration of the collective authority of the public rather than a personal one. It has to impress without being oppressive, engage without being mysterious, and excel without being exclusive. Such architecture is erected from ordinary daily life risen to splendour.

The work of Diamond and his associates is a worthy body of work in this vein, particularly in the current climate of confusion about history and the relentless search for novelty which threatens architecture with triviality. Their work stands in significant contrast in its clarity and social steadfastness of purpose.

ROOM AND CITY:
THE PRESENCE OF THE PAST

BY BRIAN CARTER

COLLEGIVM VNIVERSITATIS.

Behold, there now appears before you a handsome (speciosa) College which, since it is the species, holds by extension the name of the genus – just as in logic the species is often named for the genus and the part often comes to stand for the whole. William of Durham, a priest, gave to this one house the name of the whole city where studies are universal.[1]

This description of University College, Oxford, with its use of the terms of Latin logic, was contained in a manuscript presented to Queen Elizabeth I on her visit to the city in 1566. Not only is it a particularly original commentary on one of the more significant buildings in Oxford, but also a play on words which thoughtfully connects part and whole as well as the house, the city and the world.

The work of A.J. Diamond and Donald Schmitt demonstrates a particular preoccupation with building and the city and, whilst it is coincidental that Jack Diamond is a graduate of University College, William of Durham's vivid description of the spirit and reality of University College provides an apt reference for viewing their work. In that work and in their collaboration, these two architects have demonstrated a fierce interest in developing an architecture which addresses the definition and construction of a civilizing city. That work, completed over the last three decades, is both considerable and significant. It is also widely spread not only across Canada but farther afield, with recognized competition submissions in Europe and major public buildings which have been built in Jerusalem. Yet, almost without exception, it is work which repeatedly focuses with an increasing precision on the description of the city.

A significant amount of their attention has been directed to the city of Toronto. At its centre Toronto consists of a densely built commercial core, alongside an area of closely packed individual houses linked by distinct networks of streets, public parks and private gardens, marked by occasional monuments of industry, church and state. At its edges is an increasing spread of industry and suburb. This pattern of the city is set within and shaped by a distinctive large-scale natural landscape system formed by a series of spectacular ravines and the broad expanse of Lake Ontario. These physical patterns help to support a social framework focused on busy public streets with a mix of uses and levels of intricacy that is relatively unfamiliar in most other North American cities.

While much of the architecture is modest – a backdrop marked by occasional grander ceremonial "rooms" not unlike the drawing of University College which accompanied the description of 1566 – it provides settings for a public life developed out of European traditions but enthusiastically adopted and transformed over time by generations of Canadians. It is these characteristics which seem to be embedded in the particular interests of Diamond and Schmitt to create a truly civic architecture. It is an architecture not of objects but of spaces, of defined streets and recognizable courtyards not anonymous plazas, of carefully composed sets of urban rooms not isolated monuments.

As the part often comes to stand for the whole, so Louis Kahn claimed that "the room is the beginning of architecture."[2] That concern for the design and making of rooms has been central in the formulation of this particularly civic architecture. Diamond, who studied and worked with Kahn, has spoken eloquently of the importance of the design of the room in the planning of a house. In a discussion which started with the consideration of the window and its role in the making of a significant room, he spoke of the nature and importance of light and ventilation but went on to note the considerations of use in the shaping of a room not merely in a strictly functional sense but in the broader social context of a civilized daily life.[3]

It is these same concerns which have shaped a whole series of public rooms in the buildings that the practice has designed. So the long hall that forms the heart of the York University Student Centre creates a dignified, elegantly proportioned and carefully detailed public room befitting a space of meeting, dining and intense conversation. Unlike the drywalled transient spaces planned within the increasingly familiar homogenized environments of most urban building systems, this is a particular room clearly defined by explicit structure. The materials are substantial. Finely made in-situ concrete has been designed, formed with precision and combined with carefully selected brick in a way that imparts a considered sense of permanence fitting for the social focus of an institution of higher education. The materials are clearly expressed and obviously real – the room is exactly as it seems. Ways of moving through the space are not only obvious but generous, extending the opportunities for the social interaction that is so important in a university meeting place. The building is animated by movement, considered views and natural light, which have been carefully introduced into the scheme. Like

York University Student Centre, main dining area

others created subsequently by the same designers at Richmond Hill and in Jerusalem, this is a new room which values and reinvents familiar traditional models of the hall and meeting place, with all of the implications for social interaction, and suggests their projection onto a broader urban realm.

The examination of these rooms and their significance in this realm reveals a fundamental concern with the description of the institution and the city. The work of these designers has been consistently based on a commitment to shape fragments which denote definite ideas about an institution. They are fragments which also contribute to, and are representative of, a larger civilized and clearly legible urban whole. In striving to achieve this, Diamond and Schmitt have developed a particular interest in historic precedent and its significance for the development of a modern architecture. As the design of the room has been developed, so the potential of familiar and traditional urban forms has been explored to encourage and support a public life alongside the private place. Street, square, courtyard and garden are vital elements in the planning of their buildings, which help their shaping of the civic city through the design of the fragment. This enthusiasm for a vital urban condition is like that envisaged by Kahn when he observed that "you might say the city is actually an institution,"[4] going on to suggest that "a street wants to be a building equally organized as to space and structure as any other piece of architecture."[5] This view underscores much of the work of Diamond and Schmitt.

Without resorting to the replication of simplistic copies of traditional forms and caricature, these architects have sought to reconsider the underlying aspects of a modern architecture and its reconnection to the fundamentals of history. The Housing Union Building project, which grew out of a campus planning study prepared by A.J. Diamond and Barton Myers for the University of Alberta in Edmonton in 1976, developed student housing with commercial space and amenities for the university community which also defined a new covered pedestrian street. This street connected two heavily used but previously isolated blocks of building on a campus affected by extreme and frequently adverse weather conditions. So university life, and by implication chance meeting, informal conversation and intellectual exchange, is projected onto this new street and into the public realm. Although in a very different physical setting, this design reconstructs an idea of the street in much the same way that the university in Bologna, an institution with no buildings of its own, adopted the colonnade as its place of education.

Karl Sliva

Galleria, Housing Union Building, University of Alberta

The development of these early ideas is obvious in subsequent work. At the heart of the Metro-Central YMCA in Toronto, the design of a generous sweeping stair transforms a place of necessary linkage into a distinctive space within the building where enthusiasts, visitors or casual spectators can meet and participate in the cult and spectacle of sport. And similarly, in the development drawings and realization of both the overall plan and building detail for the new Earth Sciences Centre designed for an urban site on the campus of the University of Toronto, the reinterpretation of familiar historic forms of street, colonnade and academic court significantly shape the organization of the building to transform the view of that university and also connect it to an extended public realm in the city.

This architecture is clearly influenced by the considered organization of systems of structure and environmental servicing and of the development of design concepts through the integration of those systems. This consideration of the intricacy of the physical fabric of buildings underlines a specific concern for economy. Diamond has spoken of his architectural language as one which "is generally kept plain, with sparse and economic relief"[6] and, with the considerable direction of Donald Schmitt, this approach has been developed to inform the constructional idea and the tectonic detail as well as the conceptual approach.

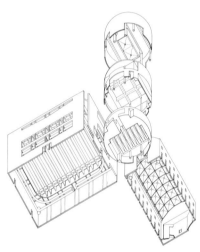

Axonometric of pool, great hall and gymnasium, Metro-Central YMCA

The buildings which Diamond and Schmitt design tend to make use of heavy and substantial materials. Perhaps this is in part a regional influence, for in southern Ontario brick, stone and concrete are familiar and carefully worked by highly skilled craftsmen. They are certainly appropriate in this climatic setting. However, the use of such materials does also introduce a sense of permanence and reality, with the *traces de la main* – the evidence of those who built them – to the buildings.

So at Richmond Hill Central Library, as both the meticulously prepared drawings and finished building readily identify, there is a distinct structural system which has been developed to make use of heavy materials precisely worked and fashioned to harbour building services. In addition, the building is planned to benefit from exposure to a southern outlook, which helps to moderate the internal conditions while at the same time explicitly defining a hierarchy of fine public rooms.

Such considerations of economy are extremely important for the development of a modern architecture which is relevant. Yet they are obviously too easily ignored as calls for limited investment and quicker paybacks direct much of today's construction into increasingly standardized systems of building and industrial production, which in turn transform architecture into a consumer item imbued with little real meaning.

The opportunity to design buildings which make fine rooms, establish the meaning of an institution, and help to build a truly civic architecture is one which is frequently offered to clients and their architects. Yet it is all too rarely seized. In scrutinizing their various commissions, Diamond and Schmitt have worked energetically with their clients and encouraged them to consider the meaning of each project in that broader context. It is a view which reiterates and reinvents the essential quality of the species and the genus in the context of the house, the city and the world. It is work which continues to create buildings that define fine spaces for the room as well as a city and establish lasting and civilizing values for both public and private institutions. It is building a truly civic architecture for a prosperous and rapidly developing society in a country committed to constructing a distinctive social democracy.

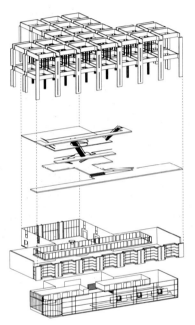

Exploded axonometric,
Richmond Hill Central Library

References

1. MS Bodley 13, pt. A. Bodleian Library, University of Oxford. University College (fol. 10 v). Translation from the Bodleian Calendar *Queen Elizabeth's Oxford, 1566* (page from September) first published for the year 1983. Adjacent image of University College, Oxford from MS. Bodley 123, fol. 10 v, University College, Oxford. Courtesy of The Bodleian Library, Oxford.

2. L.I. Kahn, "The Room, the Street and Human Agreement." June 24, 1971. Published in *a+u (Architecture and Urbanism)* 3 (1) January 1973. Page 7.

3. "Windows and Rooms: Peter Gzowski interviews A.J. Diamond." *Brick* (48) Spring 1994: 46-58.

4. L.I. Kahn. "Architecture and Human Agreement" (Lecture, University of Virginia, 18 April, 1972). Published in *Modulus*, (11) 1975. n.p.

5. L.I. Kahn. "Order in Architecture," *Perspecta. The Yale Architectural Journal* (IV) 1957: 58-65.

6. *Building with Words: Canadian Architects on Architecture.* Compiled by William Bernstein and Ruth Cawker. Toronto: Coach House Press, 1981. Page 37.

Selected Projects, 1968 – 1990

ONTARIO MEDICAL ASSOCIATION

TORONTO, ONTARIO, 1968

Second floor plan
Administration

First floor plan
Boardroom and lounge

0   5   10 m

The Ontario Medical Association headquarters is located in the Annex area of Toronto, a distinctive downtown neighbourhood filled with attractive private homes, many of them Victorian. The new headquarters' building was carefully planned to harmonize with these smaller and older structures, and to fit unobtrusively into a quiet residential street. The facade materials, setbacks, height and form of the building are similar to that of neighbouring houses.

The new building is attached to a smaller building which formerly housed all the headquarters' functions. The space between the two structures forms an interior courtyard and terrace.

The new OMA headquarters accommodates executive, administrative and social functions of the association in distinctive ways. In particular, the importance of the board of directors' role is symbolically acknowledged by assigning a circular form and central location to the boardroom. The curved wall of the boardroom is visible from the entry and the first floor lounge, which is used for dinners, receptions and other social functions. The administrative offices, located on the second and third floor, look down on the circular roof of the room, which is covered by a deck that provides an outdoor seating area for office staff.

Natural lighting was an important consideration in the design. A reverse clerestory brings light into the boardroom. Large windows on the upper floors provide both light and attractive views of the garden. High windows also illuminate the parking area, located half a level below grade.

The large windows, red quarry tile floors and exposed mechanical and electrical systems are inexpensive and ordinary building components that are used in special ways in this building to create rhythm, order and calibration of the building's spaces.

<   Boardroom, roofdeck and garden facade

St. George Street elevation

Interior detail

St. George Street entrance

Axonometric cut at third floor

HOUSING UNION BUILDING

UNIVERSITY OF ALBERTA, EDMONTON, ALBERTA 1969

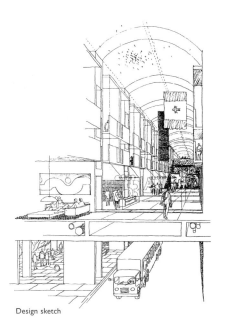

Design sketch

The HUB building, which in fact serves as the hub of the University of Alberta's Edmonton campus, was designed to meet objectives set out in the university's long range plan at a time of rapid expansion in enrollment. These objectives were: to improve the existing conditions, ensure a more cohesive form of future development, have campus facilities that house a mix of uses, and link buildings with interior public spaces to provide shelter in the severe northern climate. The students, as clients, also requested an apartment form of housing at rental rates competitive with the private market.

The design proposed two structures connected by a galleria above an existing street. While an access street is provided for vehicles, the galleria itself is free of vehicular traffic. Shopping and student recreation space are above the existing street level, with 500 apartments above that. Bedrooms are placed on the external perimeter of the building, and living rooms overlook the galleria. The building's position defines the edge of a previously undefined quadrangle.

Construction consisted of cast-in-place concrete slabs on concrete columns on both sides of the street. Connecting precast T-beams for the galleria floor and steel trusses for the continuous skylight were then set in place. Exterior walls are of precast concrete. The galleria wall is composed of glass and wood panels. Conventional methods of highrise apartment construction were adopted to build a lowrise structure within a limited construction budget.

HUB serves as a prototype for buildings designed for the extremes of the northern Canadian climate. The interior pedestrian street has become Main Street, a popular social and physical connector for the university. Its skylit galleria provides a protected interior environment for students and has knitted together housing, commercial, academic and service spaces.

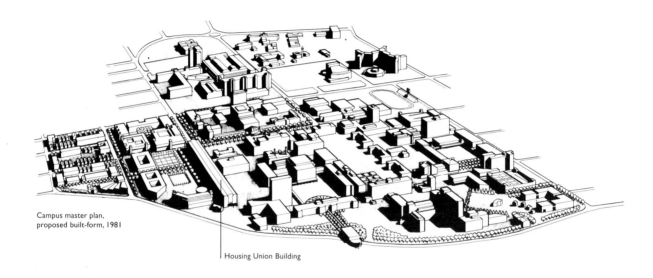

Campus master plan,
proposed built-form, 1981

Housing Union Building

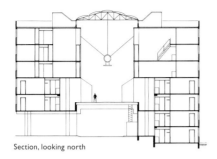

Section, looking north

Student lounge

Detail of student apartments overlooking galleria

BEVERLEY PLACE (HYDRO BLOCK)

TORONTO, ONTARIO, 1974

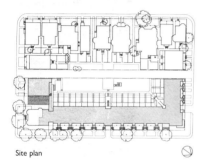

Site plan

Courtyard view, looking north

The Beverley Place project demonstrates the use of sensitive and innovative design in developing new housing that complements its neighbourhood and contributes to urban health.

In the 1960s and '70s, Toronto's diverse and vibrant urban communities were threatened by the trend toward construction of single-use residential and office towers with little sensitivity to their impact on the surrounding neighbourhood. Zoning regulations requiring that new construction provide deep setbacks and substantial parking space encouraged the trend toward highrises. Towers replaced smaller, older buildings which supported a rich mix of urban uses, including affordable housing for large and small households.

Beverley Place, earlier called the Hydro Block, is an inner-city block that was scheduled for this kind of treatment in the early 1970s. Ontario Hydro, the provincial hydroelectric corporation, announced plans to construct a 12-storey transformer station on property it had assembled in a city block midway between the Art Gallery of Ontario and the University of Toronto. But when the community raised strong objections, the site was purchased by the City of Toronto's housing company and the firm was brought in to develop a housing plan for the block.

The firm worked with area residents, inviting them to join a working committee to develop ideas about how new housing could best fit into their neighbourhood. A decision was reached to retain 12 large Victorian houses, converting them to apartments suitable for both large and small households, and to replace other, structurally unsound, buildings with a single new building.

Because the neighbourhood had convenient access to public transit and few residents had cars, setback and parking requirements were reduced. This allowed an innovative high-density, lowrise design. In effect, the highrise form was turned on its side and laid along the street, achieving a density of 80 units per acre.

The scale and design of the new building make it blend with other houses on the street, and provide a variety of apartment configurations. Two-storey units designed for larger households occupy the first two floors. Each unit has its own front door and porch opening to the street, with an individual street number. Smaller apartments geared towards singles or couples occupy the upper levels. Access to these upstairs apartments is provided by a glazed porch-like corridor which overlooks the street. The ground floor units have their own private yards and a playground area at the centre of the complex is available to all residents. Commercial space incorporates a neighbourhood café.

Beverley Place succeeded in shaping public and professional opinion. It showed that existing buildings and existing street patterns must be seen as a resource to be utilized in new developments, and that high density housing can be achieved with architecture on a human scale.

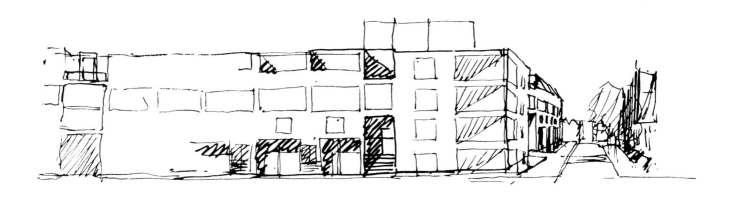

Study sketches

Study sketches

Henry Street, before

Henry Street elevation

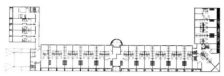

Fourth floor plan
Two bedroom apartments

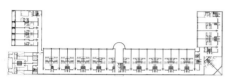

Third floor plan
Bachelor apartments

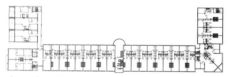

Second floor plan
Two bedroom apartments

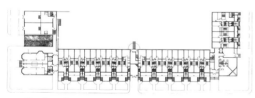

First floor plan
Upper level duplex

Ground floor plan
Lower level duplex

0 5 10 15 20 m

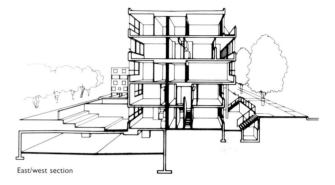

East/west section

Henry Street facade, looking south

BERKELEY CASTLE

TORONTO, ONTARIO, 1979

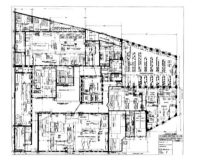

Ground floor plan of unrenovated mill complex

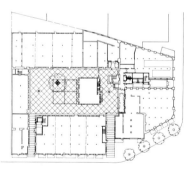

Ground floor plan renovated

0 5 10 15 20 m

Berkeley Castle is a complex renovation project in the St. Lawrence neighbourhood of downtown Toronto. It is made up of five buildings, constructed between 1868 and 1932, which originally functioned as the city's first knitting mill. While there were considerable physical problems in renovating these buildings to meet modern office building standards, the greater challenge was to create a marketable design. With the firm acting as both architect and client/developer, it was possible to control the design and the allocation of resources within a commercially based budget.

St. Lawrence Ward was a prosperous neighbourhood in the mid-1800s, and landfill was used to create an esplanade along the lakefront to accommodate new commercial and industrial enterprises. This area is where the mill buildings were built. Over time the neighbourhood declined and the buildings were used for storage.

The process of reviving the St. Lawrence neighbourhood began in the mid-1970s with plans for new housing and new uses for old buildings. This stimulated interest in the development of the old knitting mill buildings, known as Berkeley Castle. A change in zoning from industrial to mixed use, permitting residential, industrial, retail and commercial uses, was pursued.

The old buildings were condemned by the Fire Marshall in 1978. Extensive rebuilding and renovation was needed to bring the structures up to building code standards. Because of poor subsoil conditions, underground piles were needed to support new elevator shafts. Floors were leveled by truck jacks. The old wiring system was removed, and all new mechanical and electrical systems were exposed, with attention paid to their visual quality.

The focus of the plan was the development of an interior space, the old service yard, as an interior courtyard. Great effort was devoted to preserving the character of the buildings, each reflecting the style of its period of construction. The mullion divisions of the windows differed for each building and particular attention was paid to the design of new but historically complementary windows. On the interior, it was found to be less expensive to clean the brick walls than cover them with drywall. Existing wood floors were retained wherever possible, and columns and beams were stripped of paint.

Four renovated buildings surround the courtyard, with the fifth building serving as a courtyard pavilion. The courtyard is entered through arched openings. It has a lawn bordered by slate-coloured concrete paving and flower beds. The weathered brick walls, the variety of building shapes and sizes, and the courtyard give the complex a quality not offered by standard office buildings. The firm's offices are located in the complex. To acknowledge the building's industrial past, a steam whistle from a nearby factory has been installed to serve as a sound mark for the community.

Interior before restoration

Restored interior

North side of courtyard during restoration

North side of courtyard restored

METRO-CENTRAL YMCA

TORONTO, ONTARIO, 1981

Photography: Steven Evans pg. 30; Fiona Spalding Smith pgs. 32, 35, 37

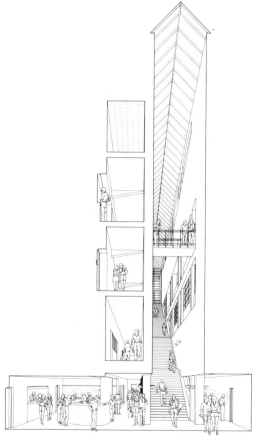

Sectional perspective of athlete's stairway

The Metro-Central YMCA building is composed of a series of functionally different and geometrically distinct forms expressive of the variety of activities it houses. It is situated on a constricted and awkwardly shaped property in downtown Toronto near the site of the former Y building, in a mixed and changing urban neighbourhood. Nearby buildings range from a modern highrise to a firehall built in English cottage style.

The YMCA is both a community service institution and a place of recreation and leisure, reflecting the organization's mission of spirit, mind and body. The downtown building serves a large and diverse population. It provides a meeting place and a broad range of programs for all ages and interests. The new building had to accommodate a childcare centre, gymnasia, a lap pool and training pool, fitness and special purpose rooms, equal changing facilities for men and women, meeting rooms, classrooms, squash and racquetball courts, running tracks and an auditorium.

The building was designed with five distinct components: double gym; swimming pools; childcare and administration; public amenities including an entrance hall, restaurant and auditorium; and space for athletic activities including squash, handball and dance.

The central location of the 300-seat auditorium represents the new Y in both its social and physical fitness functions. It is ringed with public galleries and accommodates a variety of activities by means of retractable seating and wide rollaway doors.

The sports wing is connected at each level by a skylit athlete's stairway which extends from the basement lockers to a running deck on the roof with views of Toronto's skyline. Because of tight site constraints, the indoor track is suspended below the roof and above the gymnasium floor.

The athlete's stairway demonstrates the effectiveness of using a building element for more than one purpose. In addition to providing multilevel access, it brings natural light into the building and serves as an orientation device, providing visibility and thus fostering participation in the different activities of the Y. It also serves a social purpose as a place where casual conversation can occur in the context of the many surrounding activities.

While program requirements permit few windows on the external walls, natural light is introduced to the interior via skylights over the pool and stairs and around the auditorium. Interior transparency is created by glass partitions that provide orientation and views of the many activities that take place in the building.

The training pool, located below the auditorium, has a hydraulic floor that can raise or lower the water level to suit a wide range of teaching and aquafit programs. This device also allows easy access for disabled persons. The low space of the training pool contrasts with the view into the 25-metre lap pool with its high vaulted ceiling. Coffered ceiling panels make maximum use of light and absorb sound, creating a quiet and relaxing place for swimmers.

Different structural systems of wood, steel and concrete are used for each building. The diverse program activities are articulated and distinguished by their different forms, but are made cohesive on the exterior by a consistent use of brick and stone.

In emphasizing the contrast between open and closed spaces, the design has achieved both containment and continuity, as required for program objectives and architectural aims.

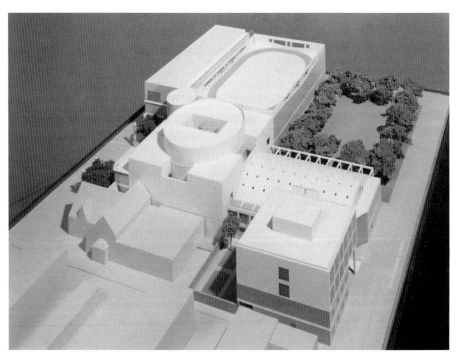

Model from northeast

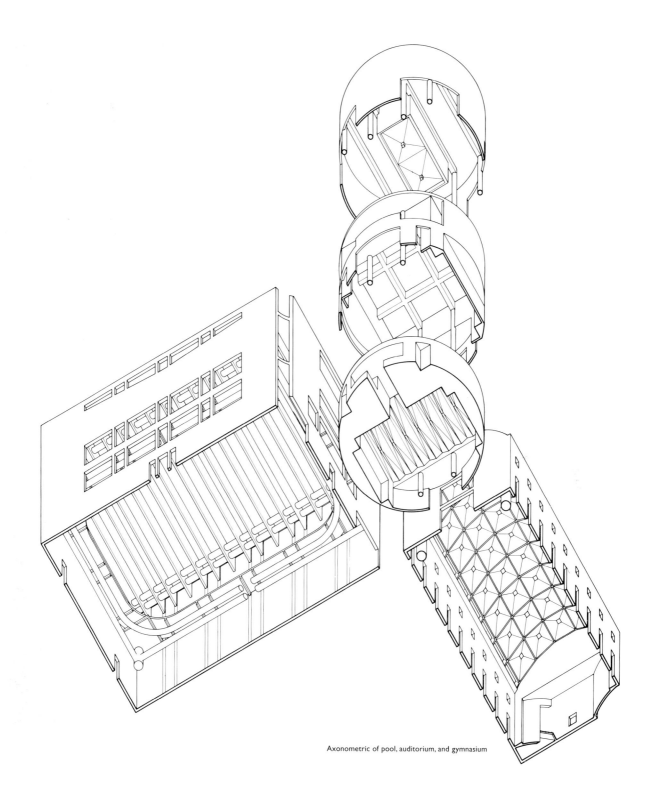

Axonometric of pool, auditorium, and gymnasium

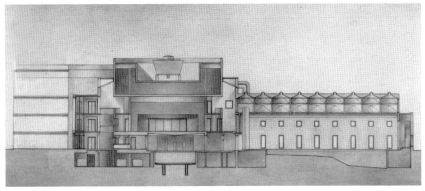

North/south section

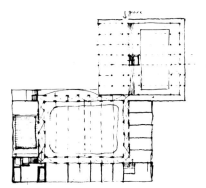

Plan studies

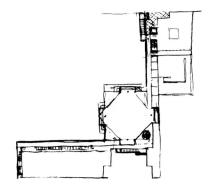

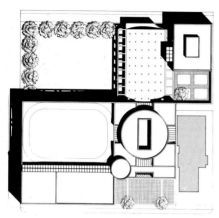

Site plan

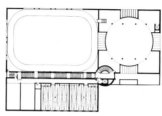

Fourth floor plan
Exercise and weight training rooms
and administration

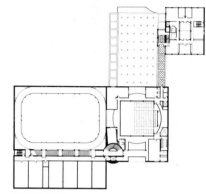

Third floor plan
Running track, squash and racquetball courts,
classrooms and administration

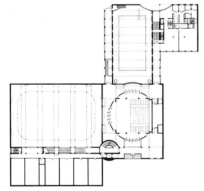

Second floor plan
Auditorium, restaurant, counselling services,
squash and racquetball courts

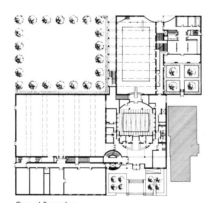

Ground floor plan
Entrance, gymnasiums, pools, day care
and exercise rooms

Basement plan
Locker rooms

0 5 10 15 20 m

Second floor multipurpose room and foyer overlooking gymnasium >

NATIONAL BALLET SCHOOL

R.A. LAIDLAW CENTRE, TORONTO, ONTARIO, 1982

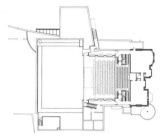

Second floor plan
Stage, auditorium and classrooms

Grade level plan
Dressing rooms, wardrobe and offices

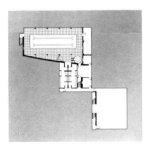

Basement level plan
Pool, physiotherapy and dance studio

0   5   10 m

The National Ballet School complex provides an environment for classroom and dance training, physical and mental rejuvenation of ballet students, as well as stage facilities to meet the needs of both students and professional dancers of world renown. It combines historic buildings and a new building with state-of-the-art technology in a way that infuses both old and new structures with meaning and vitality.

The site contained two Victorian houses of historic and architectural merit. These were incorporated into the design to provide a formal entrance to the school complex. The buildings were completely renovated to house dance studios, classrooms and administrative offices. The elaborate stone and wood facade of the Victorian buildings screens the bulk of the new building.

This building houses the Betty Oliphant Theatre, a fully equipped professional theatre with backstage facilities including a flytower. The auditorium has only 300 seats, but the stage is comparable in technical sophistication and size to major North American performance spaces. It has been equipped with specially built sprung floors, and the seating is fully retractable, allowing the space to be used for rehearsal by the National Ballet Company. Below the auditorium are a pool, physiotherapy room and whirlpool. The pool area is below grade but has skylights for natural light.

Jarvis Street elevation

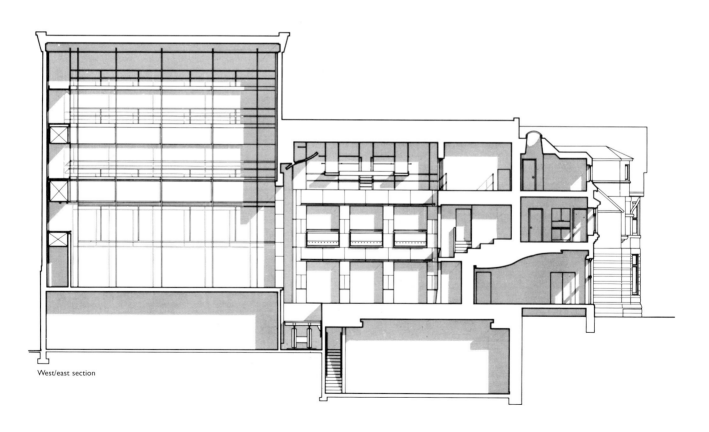

West/east section

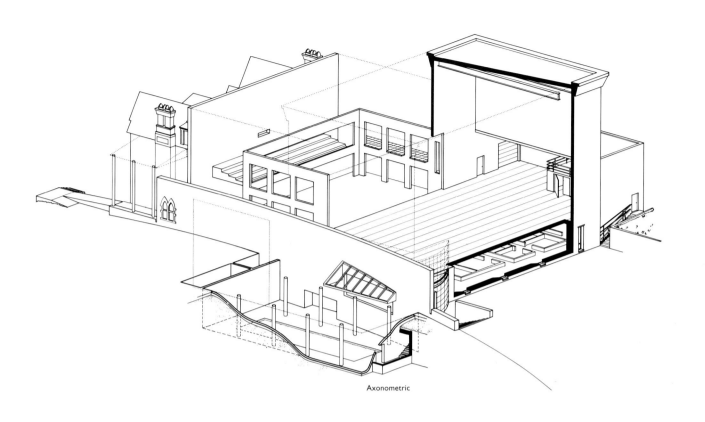

Axonometric

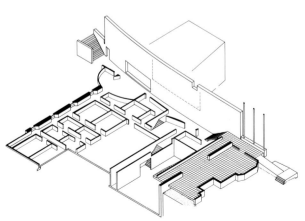

Axonometric at grade level

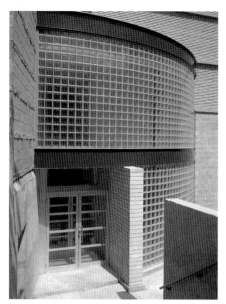

Student entrance

Pool

Auditorium screen

Flytower, stage loading,
and restored Victorian mansion >

Photography: Steven Evans

BURNS HALL OFFICERS' TRAINING FACILITY

NORTH YORK, ONTARIO, 1983

West facade

Burns Hall Officers' Training Facility, located on the grounds of an old estate in North York, is an academic facility for senior military and NATO officers. The heavily wooded site includes the original 19th century mansion and a U-shaped neo-Georgian building known as Curtis Hall. The new building, called Burns Hall, was placed next to Curtis Hall to create a new courtyard between the two structures.

Burns Hall consists of 16 syndicate rooms used for classroom instruction, a library, a computer room and a 75-seat auditorium designed to enhance the visibility of models used to teach military strategy. The building form is dominated by the 50,000-volume library located above the auditorium.

The west facade of Burns Hall is a formal entrance of buff coloured stone. The curved eastern wall, composed of glazed panels set into red brick, faces the courtyard and landscape. It encloses the main circulation space, which widens sufficiently at the centre to provide a natural gathering place. Lining its length are a high counter with a footrail, designed to encourage informal meetings and conversation. The circulation space is bracketed at each end by helical staircases.

A new tree-lined approach to Burns Hall provides a sense of arrival, improves circulation and helps demarcate the boundary along the western facade of the building, between the campus and the parking lot. The entrance lobby serves both Burns and Curtis Hall and provides an introduction appropriate to the military and academic status of the college.

Interior finishes include terrazzo, architectural concrete, steel, whitewashed concrete brick, painted gypsum board and white oak.

The new addition has become the gateway to the campus, while maintaining an unassuming relationship with the neighbourhood.

< West-facing library wall and stair tower

East facade at courtyard

Detail of library carrels – east facade

Northeast corner

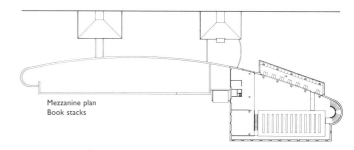

Mezzanine plan
Book stacks

East elevation

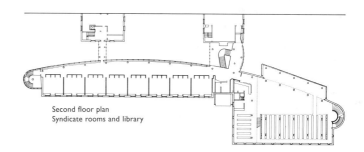

Second floor plan
Syndicate rooms and library

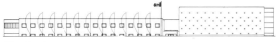

West elevation

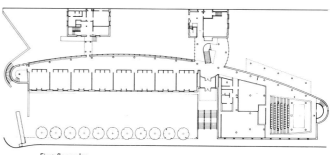

First floor plan
Syndicate rooms and theatre

0 5 10 m

North stair tower

Main corridor lounge

Library

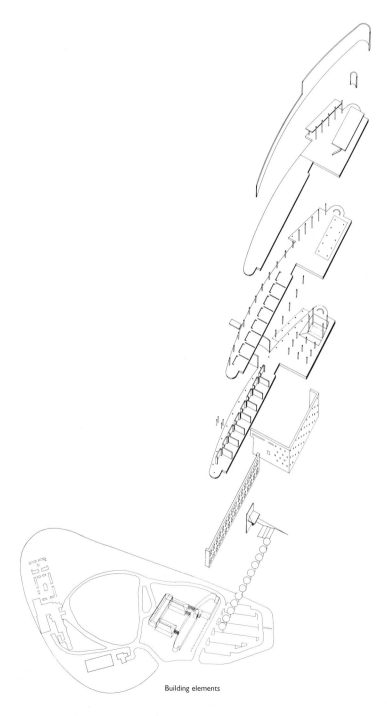
Building elements

Library mezzanine >

EARTH SCIENCES CENTRE

UNIVERSITY OF TORONTO, TORONTO, ONTARIO, 1986

North/south colonnade at Bancroft Street

The Earth Sciences Centre is a major academic and research complex providing a consolidated home for the Departments of Botany and Geology and the Faculty of Forestry. The building program includes more than 10,000 square metres of technologically advanced research laboratories, a 400-seat auditorium, lecture halls, faculty offices, student facilities and common areas. At the heart of the complex is an elliptical five-storey building containing a 125,000-volume library, a reading room and an auditorium.

The project broke new ground in the design of research and teaching facilities. The laboratories were built to modular dimensions and were serviced to allow easy adjustments to benching and equipment arrangements. Fume hoods were modified to act as a return air system, providing a greater degree of personal safety than is generally achieved. This modification also saved the cost of a ducted return air system. In contrast to most recent lab facilities, each lab and office has large windows with pleasant views of the street or courtyards.

The centre is designed to encourage interaction between students and faculty in the different academic disciplines. Research scientists consulted in the design process stressed the importance of design elements that allow opportunities to meet colleagues casually. One such element is the stairs, which are visible, convenient, have generous landings and natural light, and provide a convenient place for informal discussion.

The design has regenerated the life of the surrounding urban area and re-connected it to the campus. The use of quadrangles, courtyards and colonnades, together with buildings clad in brick and reconstructed stone, are devices employed to repair the city fabric and create a distinct academic enclave. The landscape design utilized the expertise of the Botany Department and the Forestry Faculty. The two courtyards have been planted with different regimes of plant material, thereby integrating the work of the Earth Sciences Centre and its landscape.

< Library and south courtyard

Huron Block
Laboratories and faculty offices

Library
and auditorium

Library, classrooms
and student lounge

Old Borden Dairy

Section through Huron Block and Bancroft Street elevation, south side

Old Borden Dairy

Library

Graduate student and
faculty offices (library
and auditorium beyond)

Huron Block

Russell Street elevation

North courtyard colonnade >

Stairs in Forestry wing

Library entrance stairs

Library entrance, reading room and auditorium >

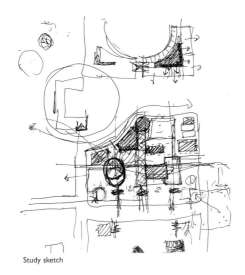

Study sketch

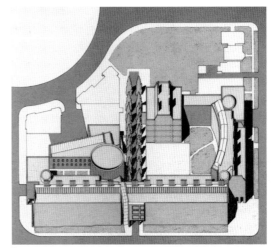

Site axonometric

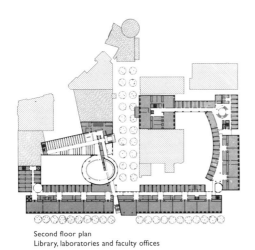

Second floor plan
Library, laboratories and faculty offices

Ground floor plan
Classrooms, auditorium, cafe, laboratories and offices

0 5 10   20m

Huron Street entrance

Library at south courtyard

NEWCASTLE TOWN HALL

BOWMANVILLE, ONTARIO, 1986

South facade of public square

Reception desk and public counters beyond

The Newcastle Town Hall consolidates municipal government facilities in a building made up of the original town hall linked to a new structure. Two aspects of civic government are acknowledged by the clear separation of functions. The historic building, designed by A.R. Denison and opened in 1904, has been renovated for council functions, and the new building houses administrative functions. The decision to retain the existing building instead of replacing it provided an opportunity to maintain historic continuity.

The renovated town hall retains the red brick and sandstone facade, large windows and cupola of the original building. The old auditorium, with its gracious proportions, generous oak staircase and balcony, is used for the formal and ceremonial functions of the corporation.

The new building has been constructed some 10 metres from the old. This arrangement allowed the creation of a new, three-storey-high atrium between the two structures which serves as a civic hall. The curved wall of this space is the project's main organizing element. It serves as both a signpost for the whole complex and a backdrop to the historic building. The cantilevered roof beams that project over the civic hall use the wall as a spine and support the office floors. The wall extends towards the downtown core, terminating in an adjacent park which is integrated with the civic centre.

The council table, balcony and a floating ceiling are placed within the restored old town hall, while the vault, core and north entrance tower can be viewed as fixed objects inserted into the new building.

The new addition is a straightforward office building with detailing that echoes the cornice, window proportions and materials of the old building. The new building is clad in red brick and has strip windows with painted metal frames, coloured precast concrete sills and a painted wood cornice. The curved wall, columns and sloped beams are structural elements made of poured concrete. Stucco is used on the triangular stair wall, vault and drum, while glazed screens are patterned with textured glass. Interior finishes include glazed block, terrazzo, carpet, perforated metal wall panels and ceilings, and stained millwork.

< North entrance and public atrium

Study elevation of north facade

South entry at public square

North facade

< New council chamber in old town hall

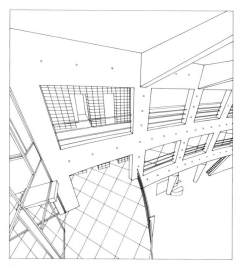

Perspective of public atrium, seen from bridge and council chamber

Perspective of public atrium looking south

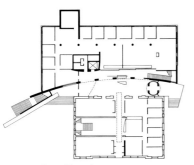

Ground floor plan
Public counters, committee rooms,
mayor and councillors offices

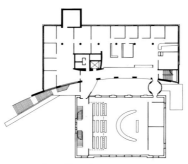

Second floor plan
Administration and public gallery

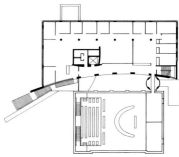

Third floor plan
Administration and council chambers

0   5   10 m

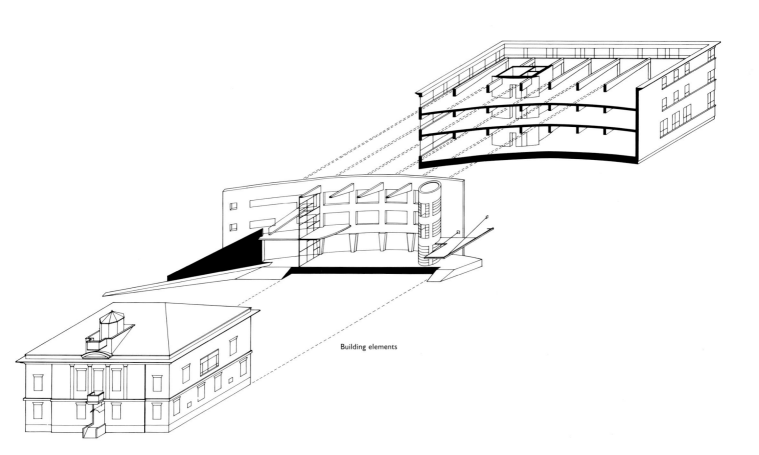

Building elements

Courtyard perspective

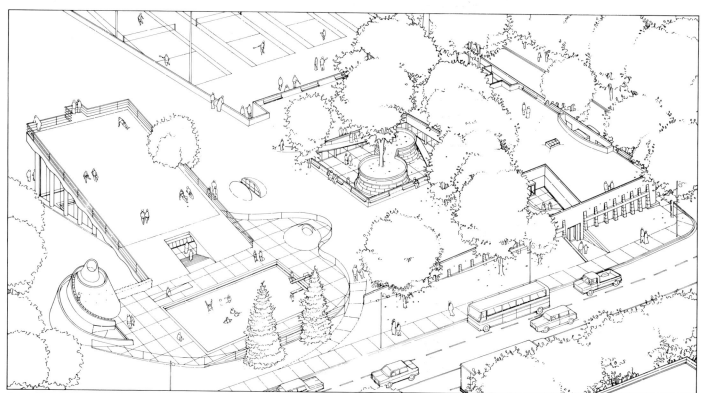

Site perspective

NORTH TORONTO COMMUNITY CENTRE

TORONTO, ONTARIO, 1987

Elevation sketch

Section sketch

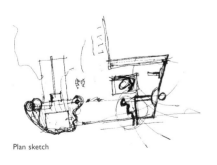
Plan sketch

When a new community centre was proposed for North Toronto, residents of the neighbourhood around the designated site were opposed to the loss of parkland which might result. Therefore, the design competition specified retention of trees as a precondition for the plan of the centre. In this shortlisted competition entry, the trees identified as significant are important design components and the site remains a park.

Because the site slopes from west to east, it was possible to build the community centre into a hill, with parkland extending over the building and supported by the roof. The centre does not feel like an underground building because the eastern end and its courtyard are exposed to natural light.

Public access through, under, and over the community centre is encouraged by a system of pathways which intersect in the central courtyard. A transverse axis from a secondary automobile drop-off extends to a winter grotto. Paths at the grotto turn to give access to the outdoor pool. The grotto's roof is designed to be used as a children's water slide in summer.

The North Toronto Community Centre project is, in a sense, a non-building. The landscape treatment and use of the site are of greater importance than the building itself. Emphasis is given to park and plant material, pathway and paving. While this entry was not selected, it influenced the design and construction of the Lois Hancey Aquatic Centre in Richmond Hill, Ontario.

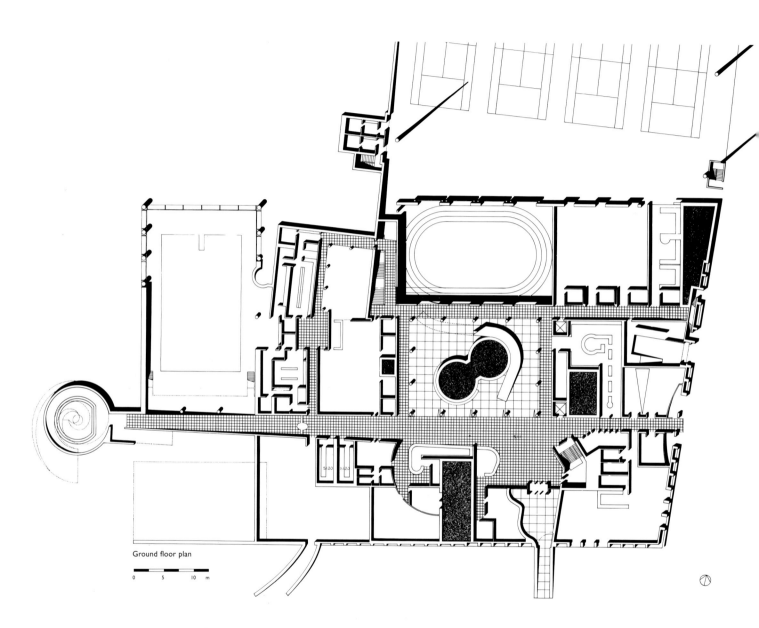

Ground floor plan

0   5   10 m

North elevation

East elevation

South elevation

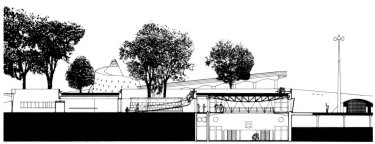

Section at gymnasium and courtyard, looking west

JERUSALEM CITY HALL

JERUSALEM, ISRAEL, 1988

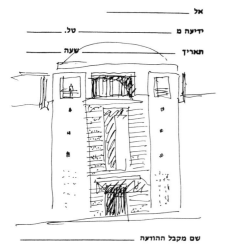

Study sketch of entrance to main building

The site for the Jerusalem City Hall complex straddles a ridge dividing the city into East and West Jerusalem. To the west is the Jaffa Road and Jewish Jerusalem. To the east is the Damascus Gate and Arab Jerusalem.

The site contained eleven buildings from a variety of periods, as well as a garden installed during the Ottoman period. The oldest buildings on the site, known as the Russian compound, were built by Tsar Nicholas II, the first European to build outside the old city walls. Other buildings were built by the French, Armenians, British, Arabs, and by Zionist settlers. One distinguished building, located beyond the site but visually an important element in the complex, is a bank designed by Erich Mendelsohn. All but one of the buildings were retained and renovated to provide space for civic departments or for commercial uses such as cafés. In all, the complex consists of ten renovated historic structures, two new buildings, three squares and four gardens.

The design addressed three main challenges. The oddly positioned collection of diverse buildings had to be used to the best urban design advantage. The new civic square had to be both contained and accessible. The new main city hall building had to be prominent without disrupting the aesthetic cohesion of the generally low-scale city, which is consistently built of Jerusalem stone.

The principal new building in the complex was located on an east-west axis where it crosses the north-south ridge, with the new domed council chamber crowning the axis. The new city square, now known as Safra Square, is located on the ridge in front of the new main building, and serves as a bridge between East and West Jerusalem.

Access to and containment of the civic square were achieved by the design of a palm grove to the west and an open bandshell to the east. On the north the square is defined by the main civic building, and on the south by a pergola. The north-south axis, anchored at the old city wall, threads through a series of renovated buildings, a small square, a triangular garden formed by the angle of the old zoological building, the pergola, Safra Square and the main lobby of the city hall building. The east-west axis,

Topographical context

anchored at the Mendelsohn building, traverses the palm court, the square, the band-shell and the ramped path down to Elisha Street. Separate but roughly parallel to the north-south axis is an aqueduct rising from an Archimedes screw in the palm court and spilling into a pool in Zahal Square. These organizing elements provide coherence to the diverse collection of buildings and open spaces. The complex is also traversed by a series of paths which provide orientation, tie the complex into the surrounding city, and reveal historic vistas.

The two new main administrative buildings were designed to create efficient office space. Both buildings and the plaza are built over an 800-car parking garage. The structure therefore had to support a number of functions as well as ensure construction simplicity. This objective was achieved using a universal 8.1-metre grid with standard 60-centimetre diameter cast-in-place columns and precast concrete slabs. Concrete block and stone cladding were used to enclose the building.

To provide an appropriate scale to the buildings on the plaza and to emphasize the pedestrian realm, the lower sections of the limestone facade were banded with alternating colours of rose and sand. These are a generous width with two 30-centimetre courses in each colour band. All metal work, including window frames, sunscreens (meshrabia), railings and light standards, is painted a traditional Arab blue.

The use of fine metalwork as a foil to the monolithic quality of the masonry is a device used effectively by the Ottomans. Limestone banding was first used to great effect by the Mamelukes in the 13th century. Other contrasts also contribute to the richness of the complex. The gardens and aqueduct associated with the informality of the cafés contrast with the geometric formality of the square and its scheduled events.

Before the new city hall complex was completed, city departments were scattered throughout Jerusalem. The new complex consolidated the civic administration offices and achieved a second significant objective – the provision of the first secular public meeting place in Jerusalem.

Elevation, main building

Temple Mount. One of a series of sketches
of the old city in preparation for design, 1988 – 1989

New main
municipal building

Stage

New east
municipal building

Renovated
Bergheim house

New municipal
building south

North/south site section

New south
municipal building

Renovated
Bergheim house

New east
municipal building

Stage

Renovated
former Russian
Consulate

New main
municipal building

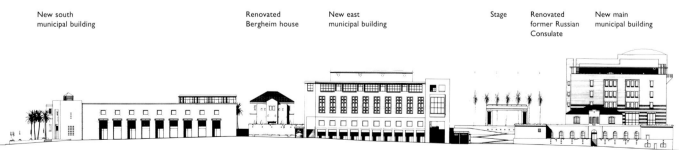

East elevation

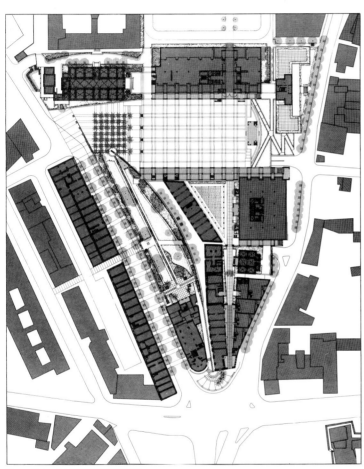

Ground floor plan of municipal complex

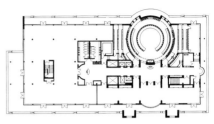

Sixth floor plan
Mayor's suite, council chamber and committee rooms

Typical floor plan, 2nd to 5th floor
Administrative office floors

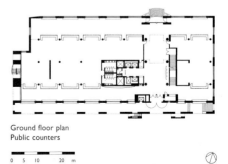

Ground floor plan
Public counters

0   5   10   20   m

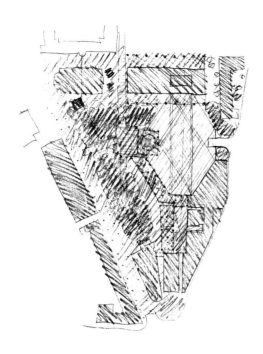

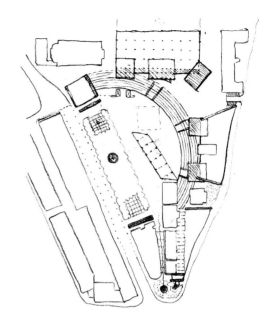

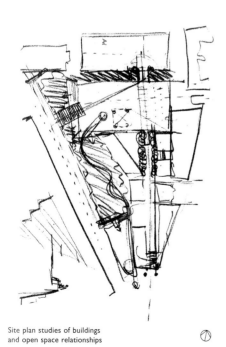

Site plan studies of buildings
and open space relationships

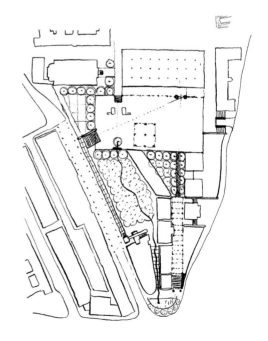

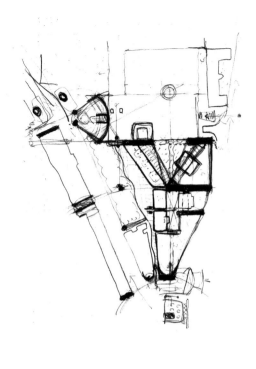

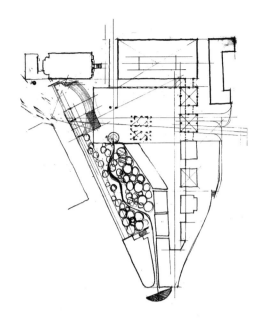

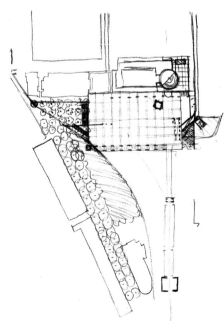

Arcade of main municipal building with view of restored former Russian Consulate

Entrance to main building with bronze ceremonial door and stainless steel inner door

View of main building through aqueduct wall

Aqueduct, cafe terrace, pergola and zoological building >

YORK UNIVERSITY STUDENT CENTRE

NORTH YORK, ONTARIO, 1988

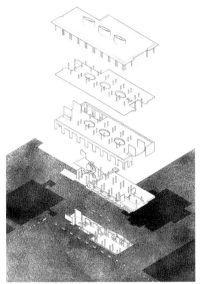

Building elements

The York University Student Centre was developed jointly by York University and the Student Centre Corporation as one of a number of projects used to implement a new master plan for the campus. The original master plan, based on suburban and modernist principles, involved freestanding buildings widely dispersed in a park-like setting.

Key considerations were the northern climatic conditions and the importance of social interaction within a university. The student centre plays a key role in the implementation of the master plan, as it creates a close relationship between buildings, provides for climate-controlled linkages, and helps to shape and define the open space of the entry green.

Since accessibility is most important in a student centre, the perimeter walkway is enclosed by triple-glazed doors that insulate the building in winter and can be stacked above head height during warmer times of the year. The inside wall of the walkway can therefore be of single glazing. This thin screen is perforated with doorways and operable windows to make the connection between campus and the building as open as possible.

The centre has two main functions. It houses entertainment and food services and provides rooms for student offices and clubs. Within both categories the centre must satisfy a wide range of requirements, such as varying degrees of accessibility or privacy. These considerations influenced the location of uses within the building. On the main entry level, food can be purchased from a variety of franchised outlets adjacent to a dining hall. Table-service dining is provided on the level below. The kitchens at the lower level also service the nearby pub and dance hall. The floors above the main entry level are filled with a series of rooms that serve as club headquarters for about 50 groups, student administration offices and reading rooms.

Three elliptical light wells penetrate the upper levels, providing natural light to rooms clustered deep in the building's interior, and to the dining areas at grade level. These large openings serve two additional purposes. They give visibility to the clubs, which serves to increase membership, and provide visible vantage points.

Structurally the building is made of a regular grid of cast-in-place columns with pre-cast concrete floors. These freestanding columns are also used to give scale and define space. Ceiling heights are varied according to the size of the rooms, to achieve appropriate proportions.

Since the building faces a very large open space, the facade was given a commensurate scale with monolithic masonry, an extended cornice and double columns uniting the two glazed upper floors. These elements also establish the student centre as a public building of some importance, while playing a role in the collective task of defining the main open space on the campus.

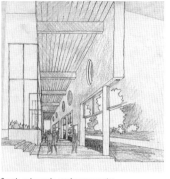

South colonnade study perspective

Model section

Model from northwest

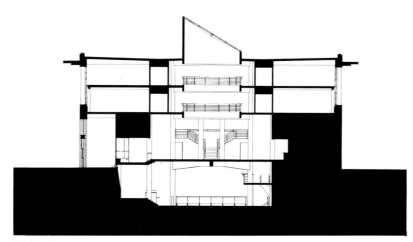

North/south section

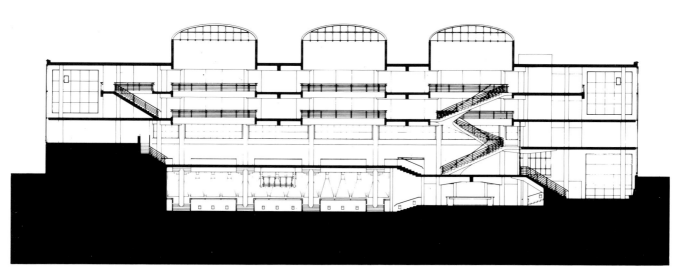

East/west section

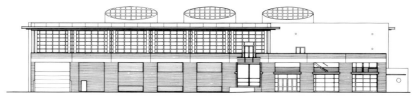

North elevation

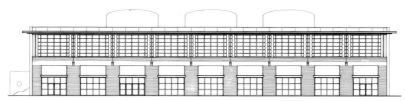

South elevation

South colonnade

Skylight detail

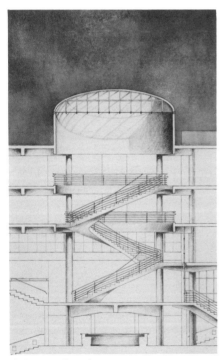

Study section of central stairway

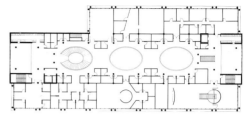

Fourth floor plan
Student clubs

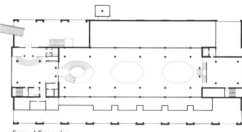

Second floor plan
Dining halls and daycare

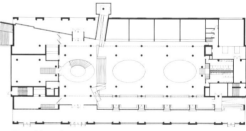

Ground floor plan
Student lounge, main dining area and art gallery

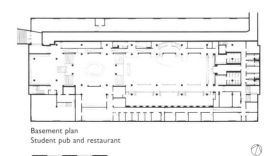

Basement plan
Student pub and restaurant

0   5   10   20   m

Mezzanine-level, student pub >

RICHMOND HILL CENTRAL LIBRARY

RICHMOND HILL, ONTARIO, 1989

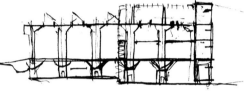

Conceptual sketch

The library is the first building to be constructed for the Richmond Hill Civic Centre complex. The 7,000-square-metre building houses 170,000 volumes and incorporates advanced library technologies. A high level of integration between structural, mechanical and electrical systems characterizes the design. The structure defines and gives appropriate proportion to the various rooms within the library, making the various functions of the library easily visible.

Light has been given much consideration in this building. While natural light is harmful to print material, it is an essential ingredient in a satisfying work environment. It is admitted, filtered, screened or blocked as appropriate to each of the library activities and spaces. Nine skylights bring light into the reference room via reflection from inverted metal cones. Each floor utilizes the natural light on the perimeter for reading and study, with perforated metal screens outside to moderate the amount of light admitted.

The building is designed to accommodate future expansion both vertically and horizontally. Another floor can be added to extend the collection and stack areas, and additional space for administrative facilities can be provided through horizontal expansion.

The exterior of the building is designed to convey permanence and solidity, symbolic of the library's role as a public institution. The protective character of the entrance colonnade conveys a sense of welcome. The design of the Richmond Hill Central Library also demonstrates the benefits of combining the definition of classical rooms with the fluidity of modern space.

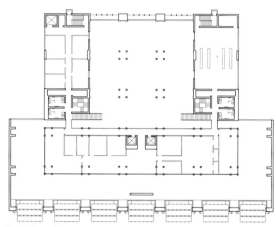

Fourth floor plan
Administration and geneology rooms

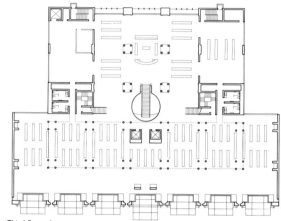

Third floor plan
Reference room, bookstacks and reading rooms

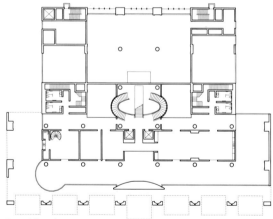

Second floor plan
Community rooms

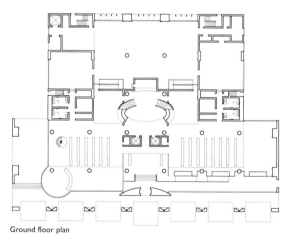

Ground floor plan
Entrance hall, circulation desk, children's library,
audiovisual library and book processing

0   5   10 m

Main reading room >

Reference table lights

Colonnade at south

Skylight screens

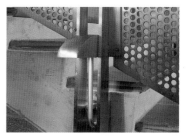
Stair light fixture

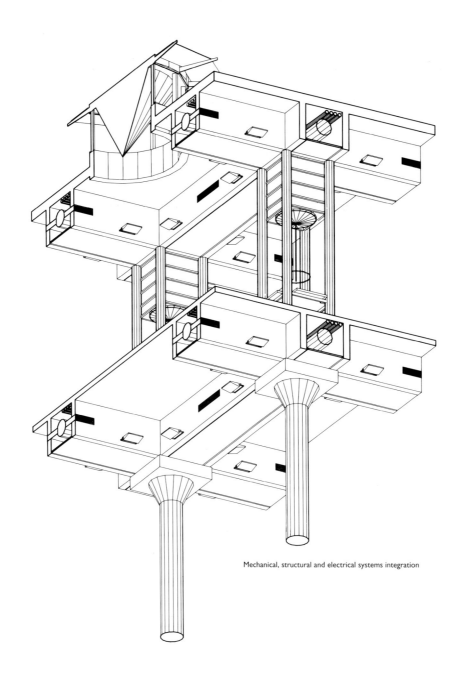

Mechanical, structural and electrical systems integration

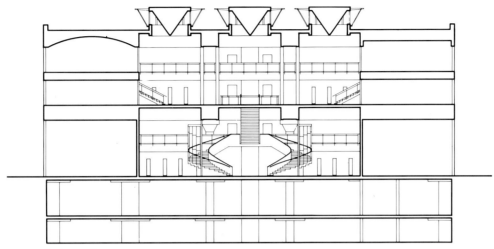

East/west section

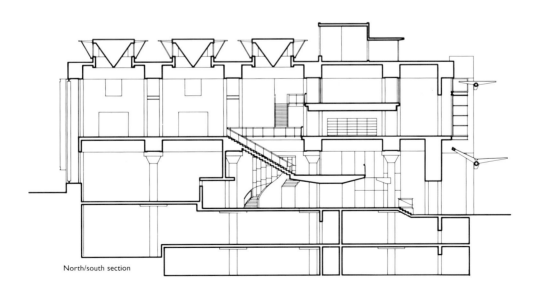

North/south section

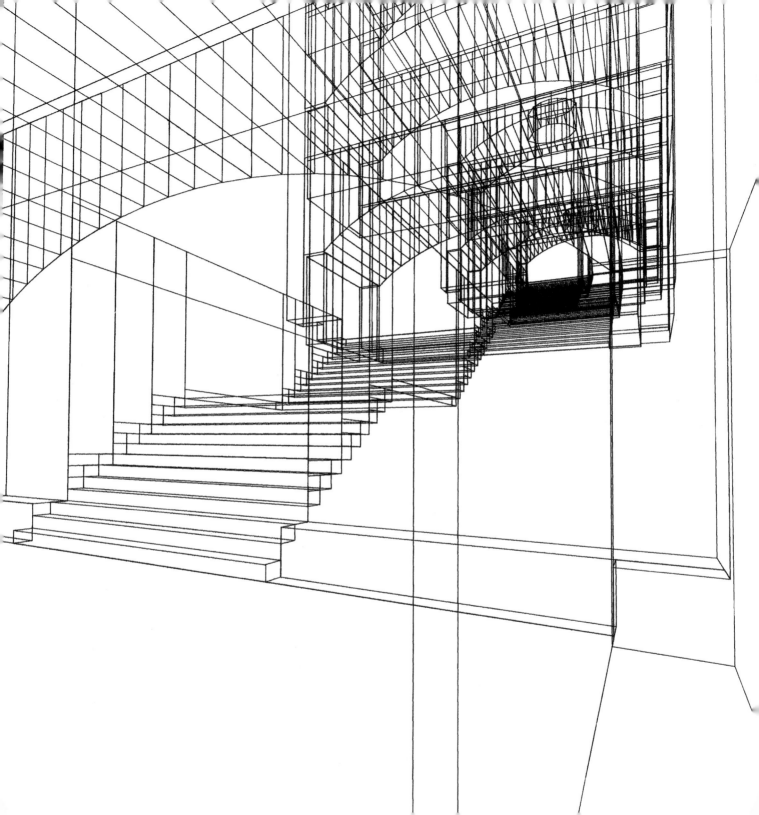

QUEEN'S UNIVERSITY LIBRARY

KINGSTON, ONTARIO, 1990

Model view from southwest

Model detail of study carrels

This design was one of four submissions in an invited competition for the new library at Queen's University. The design addresses three objectives: flexibility to accommodate future changes to the collection, clear order and orientation, and a sense of place and sanctuary for the user.

Clear orientation is achieved in a number of ways. On entering the building, the user is greeted by a plaza, a well-lit entrance lobby and the circulation desk. The circulation desk is located in a four-storey circular drum which extends the full height of the building and can be seen from the stack areas. Apertures in the top-lit space make it possible to see a number of floors at once. A frieze of authors' names, symbolic of the knowledge stored within the library, has been incorporated into the walls of the drum. Order is achieved via the central stairway, which links all floors of the building. Generous landings allow the stairs also to function as a gathering place. Services, including washrooms, copy rooms and mechanical shafts, have been accommodated within the deep enclosures to the stairs, effectively insulating quiet areas from noise.

The reading and study areas are located on the perimeter of the library, where natural light is available. Instead of using small windows or shading devices, a careful composition of various types of ultraviolet-resistant glazing was used to control and filter light.

Detailing of the library is in keeping with traditional college architecture. Carrel spaces, for example, are amalgamated into towers enclosed with glass tracery and highlighted by copper finials. The limestone cladding of the enclosing walls is in keeping with the surrounding buildings on campus.

A gentle ramp leading to the front entrance forms a forecourt, which is protected by a glass canopy and provides a place for students to sit outside during warm weather. In contrast to the hard surface of the forecourt, the historic wood frame building is set on a lawn. The design for the library also incorporates an open space on its southern side, a feature that maximizes exposure to sunlight for buildings in the northern hemisphere.

While satisfying rigorous cost and efficiency standards, the library design provides both a congenial interior atmosphere and harmony with the campus at large.

Model view of east facade

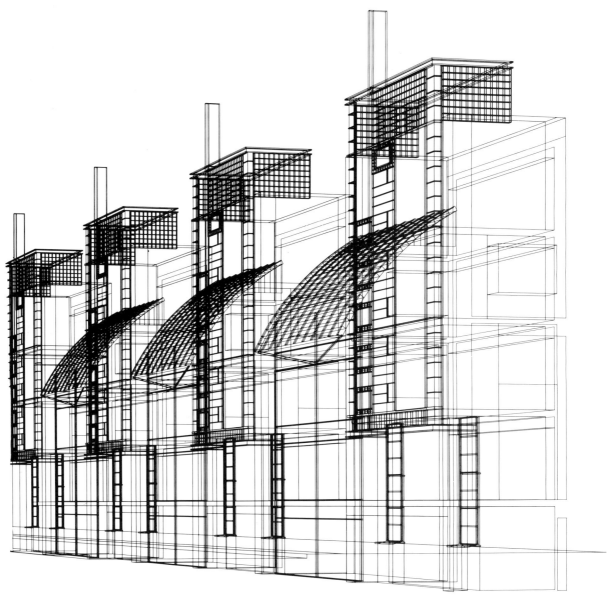

Computer wireframe of study carrels

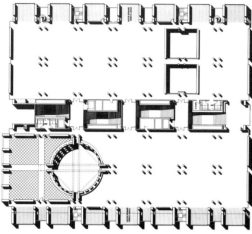

Fourth floor plan

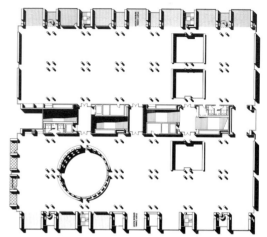

Third floor plan

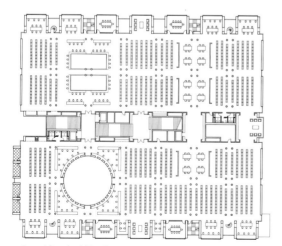

Second floor furnishing plan

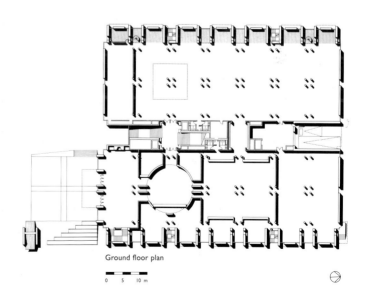

Ground floor plan

0 5 10 m

THE SANCTITY OF
CONTEXT, THE ETHIC OF TACT

BY ROBERT FULFORD

The buildings illustrated in these pages were designed during an anxious, combative time in the history of architecture, a period of spiritual turmoil. Since the 1960s, architecture has been a battleground for conflicting views of culture and history as well as of self and society. Individual projects, far from being seen as discrete artistic statements, have been recruited as foot soldiers in a war over the meaning and purposes of building itself. Increasingly, architects make strenuous efforts to develop theory that will buttress (and justify) their current practice while stimulating what they hope to do in the future. This theory may be implicit rather than explicit; sometimes it emerges only at the edges of discussion. But as they explain their work, architects inevitably reveal through their choice of language the complex web of aspirations and influences from which their designs emerge.

We can learn something about the thinking behind the buildings of A.J. Diamond, Donald Schmitt and Company from the statements their office has generated over the years in explaining their work. Certain key words and phrases appear often: "the urban fabric" in a statement on the Metro-Central YMCA, "to revitalize the campus fabric" in describing the Earth Sciences Centre at the University of Toronto, "appropriate to the residential streetscape" in the plan of Innis College, "the continuity and scale of the street... remained intact" in the scheme for the National Ballet School, "complement[ing] the existing urban context" in describing Beverley Place. Behind the tone of this prose and the favorite words – fabric, context, appropriate, and perhaps a few others that readers of this book will notice – we can discern several things: a certain deference towards the city as the architect finds it, a consistent ideology of design, and a rough outline of the ethics that govern the firm's best work.

We can find a larger context for these by briefly stepping back from architecture to consider a parallel universe of thought – political philosophy. In recent decades the theories produced by a group of philosophers – perhaps most notably the Canadian Hegelian, Charles Taylor of McGill University – have been given the name communitarianism.

This cluster of ideas focuses on the need for a way to modify liberalism's devotion to individual autonomy and "the neutral state" as the stage on which citizens act out their personal destinies. Communitarians hold that since our lives are inevitably embedded in communal practices, we derive a crucial part of our identity from community. Moreover, we should expect to act in a way that takes the community into account and should find our main goals by reference to the communal values which give us, as Taylor says, our "authoritative horizons." We discover these horizons through exploring the meaning of the communities in which we live out our lives.

Will Kymlicka of the University of Ottawa has summarized one strain of communitarian thinking: "The good for such members [of society] is found by a process of self-discovery – by achieving awareness of, and acknowledging the claims of, the various attachments they 'find'."[1] Communitarianism provides a rationale for historical and social inquiry – through study we discover the meaning of community and therefore the meaning of our lives within it. We fulfill our individual destinies only as we understand the larger scheme of which we are part. Communitarian philosophy happens to describe the process through which some of the most valuable and satisfying architecture of recent decades has been created. At the same time, the everyday research and thought involved in architecture can be seen as illustrations, also unintended, of communitarian thought. Architects look to the authority of the site, the authority of those who have used it, the practices (that is, style of buildings) that surround it. They then express in their work a sense of community derived from that environment and history. This approach to architectural practice implies that, while architects are by profession dissatisfied with the built world around them and seek to improve it, they can accomplish this central task only to the extent that they understand and respect the context in which their buildings will exist.

The Diamond and Schmitt buildings fulfill this requirement through what we might call an ethic of tact, grounded in a careful assessment of human needs. An ideal of citizenship, as opposed to a virtuoso ideal of architectural stardom, apparently governs much of what they produce. Their typical buildings seem designed to meet the urban environ-ment with skill and grace – they tend to be more humble than grand, more interested in the grammar of architecture than the rhetoric.

It is not an accident that these projects have been planned, and many of them built, in Toronto, the city that has been dominated on a certain level by the thought of Jane Jacobs. In a sense, the projects in this book illustrate the growth and elaboration of a

Jacobsian morality that strains to encompass both the needs of the spontaneous self and the requirements of a rooted community – and capitalizes on the interplay and creative conflict between the two.

Two projects that are superficially different, York Square and Berkeley Castle – a commercial centre and a group of industrial buildings recreated as offices – are significantly alike. Each successfully establishes its own environment, yet each honours the larger environment in which it is placed. Each of them, with its thoughtful integration of diverse elements, can also be read as illustrations of a remark by Louis Kahn: "Integration is the way of nature. We can learn from nature."[2] Another notable Toronto achievement of recent decades, not formally connected to the firm itself, deserves to be mentioned in this connection. The vast St. Lawrence Neighbourhood, built in the late 1970s in the southeast corner of downtown Toronto, owes a great deal (as its planners have acknowledged) to A.J. Diamond's practice and advocacy. It plays out on a large scale Diamond's use of "infill" architecture as a solution to some of the inherent problems of evolving cities.

The best of the Diamond and Schmitt buildings exhibit graceful proportions, a coherent resolution of design problems, and a degree of originality. What links them to each other is the same element that unites them with their communities: an overarching sense of the sanctity of context.

References

1. *Contemporary Political Philosophy: An Introduction.* Oxford: Oxford University Press, 1990, page 213.

2. Ockman, Joan, ed., *Architecture Culture 1943 – 1968: A Documentary Anthology,*
   New York: Columbia University Press, 1993, page 272.

Chronological Index of

Buildings and Projects, 1968 – 1995

CHRONOLOGICAL INDEX OF
BUILDINGS AND PROJECTS, 1968 – 1995

1968

ONTARIO MEDICAL ASSOCIATION
Toronto, Ontario
(Diamond and Myers)

see page 13

YORK SQUARE
Toronto, Ontario

This project set a precedent for Toronto in terms of building renovation, urban infill and creating a mid-block courtyard. Renovated 19th century houses were combined with new construction to form a tree-shaded courtyard in the former backyards of the houses.

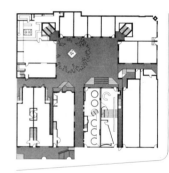

1969

ALCAN PRODUCTS HEAD OFFICE
Toronto, Ontario
(Diamond and Myers)

Two floors of the Royal Trust Tower designed by Mies Van der Rohe were fitted out for corporate offices. The plan was devised to optimize daylight, views of the city and interoffice communication for all employees. Aluminum was used both as a finishing material and in details, using stock extrusions.

LONG RANGE DEVELOPMENT PLAN
UNIVERSITY OF ALBERTA
Edmonton, Alberta
(Diamond and Myers, revised 1980 by A.J. Diamond Associates)

The long range plan was developed to meet the university's needs for new buildings within the existing campus to accommodate growth and provide climate-controlled linkages between campus facilities for shelter in the harsh Edmonton climate. The plan also shapes exterior spaces.

HOUSING UNION BUILDING
UNIVERSITY OF ALBERTA
Edmonton, Alberta
(Diamond and Myers)

see page 17

Karl Silva

1970

ECLIPSE WHITEWEAR BUILDING
Toronto, Ontario
(Diamond and Myers)

The renovation and conversion of 19th century mill-construction warehouses for office use employed a vocabulary of stock electrical and mechanical components as new elements of architecture within the exposed wood and brick structure.

Ian Samson

1973

CITADEL THEATRE
Edmonton, Alberta
(Diamond and Myers in association with R.L. Wilken Architect)

The Citadel Theatre, commissioned as the result of a design competition, is situated above an existing parking structure and absorbs an existing pedestrian mall within its lobby. The principal 700-seat proscenium theatre, 300-seat experimental theatre and 250-seat cinema/lecture hall are surrounded by glazed lobbies. These public spaces create a dramatic and transparent link with the surrounding city.

John Fulkerr

DUNDAS-SHERBOURNE HOUSING
Toronto, Ontario
(Diamond and Myers)

This project demonstrated the effectiveness of lowrise, high density housing. The buildings, built along laneways behind 19th century houses, retain the scale of the neighborhood, but the project density is equivalent to that of a highrise tower.

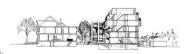

BEVERLEY PLACE (HYDRO BLOCK)
Toronto, Ontario
(Diamond and Myers)

see page 21

Karl Sliva

INNIS COLLEGE
University of Toronto
Toronto, Ontario

The College incorporates an existing 19th century house with new buildings housing an auditorium, library, seminar rooms and faculty offices. The new buildings retain the scale and continuity of the streetscape. The intention was to reinforce an existing neighbourhood and meet the needs of a university college.

Ian Samson

1975

QUEEN STREET
MENTAL HEALTH CENTRE
Toronto, Ontario

The master plan demonstrated the feasibility of renovating the provincial asylum, designed in 1846 by John Howard, to accommodate the modern requirements of a psychiatric hospital. Although it demonstrated that renovation would cost less than new construction, the provincial government decided to demolish the asylum, a designated heritage landmark, in 1976.

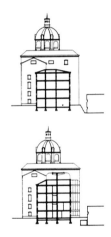

STUDENT HOUSING
Queen's University
Kingston, Ontario

A master plan was developed to renovate turn-of-the-century single-family houses for student accommodation and to create new residences by filling in the vacant lots between the houses. Three existing row houses were renovated to provide suites for ten students.

A.J. Diamond

VILLAGE TERRACE
Toronto, Ontario

The apartment tower mediates between the highrise towers immediately to its east and the lowrise neighbourhood and ravine to the west. The building is a hybrid incorporating a point tower, stepped terrace apartments and two-storey row houses with private gardens at its base. The building is unified by a monolithic skin of red clay brick and similarly coloured morter.

Fiona Spalding-Smith

GERRARD STREET PUBLIC LIBRARY
Toronto, Ontario

As an addition to an existing two-storey library with pitched roof and dormers, the design integrated contemporary architecture with the tradition of the original building design. The addition aligned the front of the library with the shops along Main Street.

LEBRETON FLATS NEIGHBORHOOD PLAN
Ottawa, Ontario

A neighbourhood plan was developed to house 12,000 people on a 100-acre site on the Ottawa River west of Parliament Hill. The plan extends the urban structure of the adjacent city, accommodates the Parkway and rapid transit systems and provides a site for ceremonial functions of the nation's capital. A series of canals and landscape features are incorporated in the plan.

UNION STATION MASTER PLAN
Toronto, Ontario

The study demonstrated that Union Station could both provide for the long-term transportation needs of the city and accommodate additional real-estate development.

ALCAN SMELTERS AND CHEMICALS LTD.
Montreal, Quebec

This project inverted the conventional office planning model of enclosed offices at the building perimeter and open work-stations and offices on the interior. Offices requiring acoustic privacy are placed on the interior with glazed partitions. Departmental circulation and open work-stations are distributed along the glass perimeter, making views and natural light available to all.

Fiona Spalding-Smith

ARVIDA MEDICAL CLINIC
Arvida, Quebec

The clinic provides health services for 6000 Alcan employees. Its four departments – emergency, medical testing, medical consultation and administrative services – are clustered around a skylit interior court. The building is clad in delicately ribbed aluminum truck siding fastened with exposed neoprene bolts.

Fiona Spalding-Smith

BERKELEY CASTLE
Toronto, Ontario
see page 27

1980

BURNS BUILDING
Calgary, Alberta
(with Gerald Forseth Architect)

The original headquarters of the Burns
Meat Packing Company, constructed
in 1913, was renovated and extended.
The white terra-cotta facade of the old
building was restored, and new glazing
and mechanical services were installed.
The addition, built with contemporary
technology and materials but using
an identical floor plan, is in harmony
with the old.

Lenscape

**WOODSTOCK LIBRARY
AND ART GALLERY**
Woodstock, Ontario

A plan was devised to double the size
of the historically designated Carnegie
Library, circa 1909. A new wing was
designed to house an expanded adult
library, a children's library, an audiovisual department and a city art gallery.

1981

**ALCAN ALUMINUM
CORPORATION LTD.**
Cleveland, Ohio

This office interior, on the thirtieth
floor of Cleveland's Erieview Plaza,
accommodates senior executive offices
and the workstations of senior staff
around the building perimeter. The
reception desks, conference tables and
interior details were designed with
white marble, black slate, aluminum
and sandblasted glass.

Fiona Spalding-Smith

METRO-CENTRAL YMCA
Toronto, Ontario
see page 31

SPADINA QUAY
DEVELOPMENT COMPETITION
Toronto, Ontario

The buildings in this proposal were planned both for tenant satisfaction and to shape the sequence of parks, squares and gardens that form the open spaces of the neighbourhood. The various buildings were not designed in isolation but in relation to each other, giving shape and coherence to the water-front community.

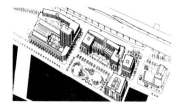

UNIVERSITY OF ALBERTA
LONG RANGE PLAN
Edmonton, Alberta

The firm was retained to update the Long Range Development Plan. The plan provided design guidelines and specific policies controlling campus circulation to direct physical improvements and developments on campus from 1981 to 1991. The plan proposes an open space system of quadrangles and landscaped walkways as well as indoor pedestrian links throughout the campus.

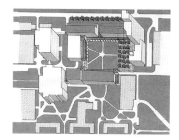

1982

410 BLOOR STREET EAST
Toronto, Ontario

This apartment tower was designed for a narrow site between Bloor Street and the Rosedale Valley. The base is clad in red brick and Ontario stone, in keeping with the adjacent bank designed in 1911 by John Lyle. The rectangularity of the street elevation contrasts with the curvilinear glass wall of the north facade, as viewed from the ravine to the north and through the trees from the Sherbourne Street Bridge.

Lenscape

NATIONAL BALLET SCHOOL
R. A. LAIDLAW CENTRE
Toronto, Ontario

see page 39

1983

BURNS HALL OFFICERS'
TRAINING FACILITY
North York, Ontario

see page 45

LA TÊTE DEFENSE COMPETITION
Paris, France

A series of building forms, including a circular highrise office and apartment tower, a gridded communication marketplace and spherical auditoria were designed in the context of the modernist La Tête Defense precinct.
The site is at the western limit of the Champs Elysées and is bounded by the auto-route périphérique.

VILLAGE GATE APARTMENTS
Toronto, Ontario

A six-storey apartment building encloses three sides of a garden court and pool. The building consists of a variety of unit types: two-storey town houses with individual garden courts at grade, conventional double-loaded apartments on the upper floors, and terraced penthouse units on the roof.

1984

**CANADIAN STAGE
COMPANY MASTER PLAN**
Toronto, Ontario

The master plan fitted out a 19th century complex for theatre uses. The existing structure was used for two small theatres, public foyers and support facilities, while a new structure was designed to house a flexible 900-seat theatre. Phase one of the master plan has been implemented.

**FOUR SEASONS HOTELS
HEAD OFFICES**
Don Mills, Ontario

A 40,000-square-foot single-storey industrial plant was renovated to provide corporate offices. A courtyard was created to bring natural light and views to meeting rooms, reception and dining facilities.

JAPAN RESTAURANT CENTRE
Toronto, Ontario

The building was designed for a Japanese client to house seven restaurants, each with a distinct identity appropriate for a different Japanese cuisine.

NEAR EAST SIDE PLANNING STUDY
Dallas, Texas

The future of this derelict industrial area adjacent to the downtown core was in doubt. The plan established appropriate densities and land uses, utilizing the industrial buildings and location to advantage.

OAKLAWN PLANNING STUDY
Dallas, Texas

The Oaklawn district lies between a stable upper-income residential area and the commercial core of Dallas. Subject to development pressures, conflicts arose between developers, retailers and homeowners. The plan, adopted by City Council, resolved the conflicts and established a framework for change that preserved the attractive low-scale characteristics of the area while accommodating new development.

ROYAL OPERA HOUSE COMPETITION
Covent Garden, London

This short-listed design in an open international competition for the expansion and renovation of Sir Charles Barry's Opera House included a new stage and back-of-house facilities, the expansion of public lobbies and the reconstruction of the 19th century Floral Hall, giving the opera house a presence on Covent Garden Square. Part of this scheme was to include a revenue-producing retail and office building.

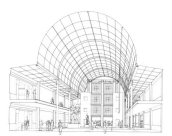

1985

ARCADIA HOUSING CO-OPERATIVE
Toronto, Ontario

In designing these apartments to provide both living and working space for artists, the objective was to provide interior flexibility at the lowest cost possible. The south-facing apartments are wide, with 3-metre-high ceilings, tall windows and balconies for sun protection. The north-facing units are narrow two-storey units with double-height studios and large windows.

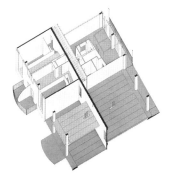

BLOOR YORKVILLE DISTRICT URBAN DESIGN MASTER PLAN
Toronto, Ontario

The plan establishes consistent guidelines for landscape, street furniture and signage for this 27-block urban neighbourhood. The distinctive lamp standard and signage provide clear identity to the district.

AJD / DS office

GEORGE HEES WING SUNNYBROOK HEALTH SCIENCE CENTRE
Toronto, Ontario

This 270-bed facility redefines the way institutions for long-term care serve both residents and the public. The residential wing is self contained and built around a garden courtyard, ensuring privacy and controlled access. Among other amenities the south wing has a two-storey living room and a community centre for the use of both residents and visitors.

ART GALLERY OF ONTARIO
PHASE III EXPANSION
COMPETITION
Toronto, Ontario

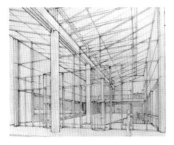

A granite-paved public walk extends
from the 19th century landscape of
Grange Park past Grange House, which
is maintained as a freestanding pavilion,
and then into the gallery. The walk
traverses an outdoor terrace which provides access to the gallery and all its
public and retail services, and termi-
nates at an entry court on Dundas
Street. Sculpture galleries and the
Walker Court atrium beyond are visible
through large gallery windows on
Dundas Street.

EARTH SCIENCES CENTRE
UNIVERSITY OF TORONTO
Toronto, Ontario
(with Bregman and
Hamann Architects Ltd.)
see page 51

FRONT STREET MARKET
COMPETITION
Toronto, Ontario

This competition entry for an apartment
tower and market located in the city's
St. Lawrence neighbourhood included
the design for a building located opposite
to the Gooderham Building, an existing
19th century flat-iron building, and
similar in form to it.

HOTEL, TEL AVIV
Tel Aviv, Israel

Every unit in this all-suite hotel is
planned with a view of the ocean. The
suites enclose a garden court which has
a four-storey opening facing the ocean.

JESSIE'S CENTRE FOR TEENAGERS
Toronto, Ontario

The building houses a centre for the
care, nurturing, counseling and tempo-
rary accommodation of single mothers
and their children. The upper four
floors provide two and four bedroom
apartments.

MASONRY DESIGN
CENTRE COMPETITION
Mississauga, Ontario

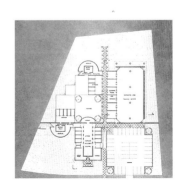

The centre was designed to house trade
associations and accommodate appren-
tice training in a campus of separate
buildings linked by colonnades and
pergolas, with a variety of gardens and
a parking court. The best attributes of
traditional masonry methods, assem-
blies and patterns are demonstrated in
the design.

**MOUNTAIN VIEW CIVIC
CENTRE COMPETITION**
Mountainview, California
(with Tanner Van Dyne Architects)

Built around an existing mature park,
the plan for a new civic plaza unites a
new theatre to the south, the city hall
and council pavilion to the north, the
park to the west and Castro Street to
the east. Layered trellises, sunscreens
and planting shade the building along
the long south facade.

NEWCASTLE TOWN HALL
Bowmanville, Ontario

see page 59

**"PLANNING YOUR
LIBRARY BUILDING"**
Ministry of Culture,
Tourism and Recreation
Province of Ontario

Written for libraries, library boards
and architects, the guidebook outlines
library planning and design processes.

POINTE À CARCY COMPETITION
Quebec City, Quebec

This design, selected by competition
but not built, proposes a mixed-use
neighborhood that would extend the
scale and structure of the adjacent
quartier Place Royale onto a largely
vacant riverfront site. The historic
Customs House and existing amphitheatre are framed by a new square
which protects pedestrians from winter
winds off the St. Lawrence River.

**SHAAREH HAIM
SYNAGOGUE AND SCHOOL**
Richmond Hill, Ontario

A small group of linked buildings, each
with a separate identity, house the sanctuary, chapel and entrance hall. Classrooms, administrative offices, gym,
banquet and kitchen facilities are
housed in a simple building which
encloses the courtyard. Only the
primary school has been built.

**TERMINAL WAREHOUSE
CONVERSION COMPETITION**
Toronto, Ontario

While maintaining the scale, character
and major elements of the existing
warehouse, the design introduced
retail, office, parking and residential
uses to this enormous building.
Apartments, offices and shops are
arranged around the building perimeter, with atria and parking at the centre, and a garden court on the rooftop.

CABLE BEACH HOUSING
Nassau, Bahamas

One hundred houses are arranged around three courtyards, the largest of which is a tropical garden opening to the beach and ocean. An existing villa in the neoclassical style, flanked by new pavilions, serves as a clubhouse for the residents.

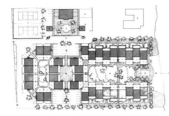

CANADIAN CLAY AND GLASS MUSEUM COMPETITION
Waterloo, Ontario

The museum occupies a pivotal point between the city centre and adjacent park system. The plan is composed of a series of public rooms arranged along a display wall, beginning on land and extending over Silver Lake to the galleries. Administrative and service areas, on a perpendicular axis, contain the park edge and support a lawn and terrace overlooking the lake.

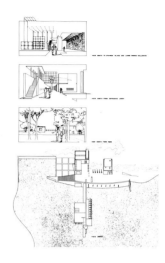

HAZELTON LANES PHASE TWO
Toronto, Ontario

The building provides six floors of apartments above a two-level retail mall. The east-facing apartments follow the line of an arc, a configuration which reduces the apparent length of the corridor, creates distinct suite entrances and defines a garden at podium level. The units facing west are stepped in an orthogonal plan providing long street views from bay windows.

LOIS HANCEY AQUATIC CENTRE
Richmond Hill, Ontario

The centre is built into a site which slopes steeply to the south, with parkland on the north side that extends onto the roof. From the north only the skylights are visible. From the south the building facade reveals the main entrance and large windows. Contained within are a wave pool, water slide, rainmaking equipment, spa and fixed lanes for endurance training, as well as a childcare centre, snack bar and locker rooms.

NORTH TORONTO COMMUNITY CENTRE COMPETITION
Toronto, Ontario

see page 65

OLYMPIC ARCH
Calgary, Alberta

Winner of a national competition, this sculpture is composed of a group of eight athletes supporting a parabolic arch, symbolizing the Olympic ideal of teamwork. The athletes were cast life-size in bronze by Colette Whiten.

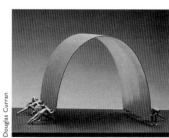

Douglas Curran

STUDENT SOCIAL CENTRE
McMaster University,
Hamilton, Ontario

The design defined a way to convert the old drill hall into a dance hall and pub for 1000 students. An upper mezzanine, under exposed heavy timber trusses, accommodates alcoves for seating and support spaces.

1988

**BATHURST-ST. CLAIR
RESIDENTIAL COMPETITION**
Toronto, Ontario

The program brief was to accommodate over a million square feet of primarily residential development. The competition design proposed four towers united by lowrise buildings which define a public street. The project could be built in three separate phases.

JERUSALEM CITY HALL
Jerusalem, Israel
(in association with
Kolker Kolker Epstein Architects,
Meltzer Igra Architects and
Bugod Figueiredo Niv-Krendel Architects)

see page 69

SIMPLICITY HOUSE
*Mustique, St. Vincent
and the Grenadines*

Each room of this house is itself a building. These pavilions are sited to take advantage of the sea breeze and panoramic views, and to provide privacy. A courtyard, enclosed by a long retaining wall, provides a focus to the complex and is the social centre of the house.

Tim Griffiths

YORK UNIVERSITY STUDENT CENTRE
North York, Ontario

see page 81

1989

ATARATIRI NEIGHBOURHOOD
Toronto, Ontario

Two urban design options were prepared to shape a new downtown neighbourhood for 12,000 people on 65 acres of unused industrial land adjacent to the Don River.

CENTREPOINTE OFFICE AND RESIDENTIAL DEVELOPMENT
Toronto, Ontario
(with Page and Steele Architects and Planners)

This large mixed-use development, in a strategic location adjacent to Union Station, retained the historically and architecturally important Art Deco Canada Post building. Grade and below-grade links to the railroad terminal and the city's underground walkways were the basis of the urban design and public space system.

RICHMOND HILL CENTRAL LIBRARY
Richmond Hill, Ontario
(with Richmond Hill Civic Centre Architects)

see page 89

TORONTO POWER GENERATING STATION CONVERSION STUDY
Niagara Falls, Ontario

The hydroelectric station, built in 1913 by Sir Henry Pellatt, has been vacant since it was closed down in 1974. In response to a proposal to demolish the building and create a "classical" ruin in the park, the firm produced an alternative renovation scheme utilizing the entire building as an interpretive centre about electric power and the industrial development of the Niagara Gorge.

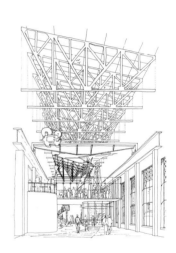

1990

1319 BAY STREET
Toronto, Ontario

A small 12-storey tower with 400 square meters per floor accommodates one apartment on each floor. A two-storey penthouse with views to the east, south and west caps the building.

BATHURST/LAWRENCE APARTMENT BUILDING
North York, Ontario

Ninety apartments are accommodated in a six-storey building on a main arterial street. The facade is articulated as a terrace block with a deeply modeled, repetitive sequence of glass and masonry bays.

GOODERHAM & WORTS HERITAGE INDUSTRIAL LANDS REDEVELOPMENT MASTER PLAN
Toronto, Ontario

The distillery is one of the finest, most complete and well maintained examples of 19th century industrial architecture in North America and is a National Historic Site. The plan outlined the principles for redeveloping the site economically, integrating residential, commercial, retail and institutional uses in an appropriate manner.

QUEEN'S UNIVERSITY LIBRARY
Kingston, Ontario

see page 97

1991

BASTION STE. ANNE
Beaune, France

A garden dating from the 14th century is contained within the rampart walls of the Ville de Beaune. The existing two-storey pavilion and its greenhouse are to be restored and the garden orchard re-established.

BRONTE HARBOUR WATERFRONT PARK
Oakville, Ontario

The plan provides for a new lakefront park and the expansion of marina services in an outer harbour created by landfill. The focus of the park is an amphitheatre surrounded by formal gardens, a boat display basin and a large water jet. The plan of the park takes account of the city grid, thereby reintegrating the city with its waterfront.

CUMBERLAND PARK COMPETITION
Toronto, Ontario

The competition design was based on the principle that the park should function as a self-sustaining ecology. The design employed a number of devices to reveal both the natural and urban history of the site.

ETOBICOKE WATERFRONT MASTER PLAN
Etobicoke, Ontario

The plan was commissioned by the Province of Ontario in response to uncoordinated highrise development proposals. The plan established a grid of public streets which provides access to the edge of Lake Ontario and defines the structure of a well integrated neighbourhood. The built form of the complex accommodates 2700 apartment units that step up from four storeys on the waterfront to twelve storeys along the adjacent arterial road.

GREAT LAKES SCIENCE CENTRE
Burlington, Ontario

The centre, located at the entrance to Hamilton Harbour, will act as a forum for research about water quality issues and environmental technology. It will also act as a learning centre, informing the public of the geography, history and future of the Great Lakes area, which contains one-fifth of the world's fresh water supply.

HALTON REGION TRANSIT OPPORTUNITIES STUDY
Halton Region, Ontario
(with McCormick Rankin Engineers Ltd.)

The study defined the long-term policy and strategies that regional governments should adopt to support expanded transit services and future growth. The study proposed that development be shaped by the symbiotic relationship between land use, density and transportation, and demonstrated the need for comprehensive and phased transit planning.

ST. MICHAEL'S COLLEGE LANDS DEVELOPMENT
Toronto, Ontario

A residential development of 640 apartment units was designed at the eastern edge of the University of Toronto's St. Michael's College lands, adjacent to St. Basil's Church. The buildings define the urban boundary between the city and the university.

SEAGRAM LANDS DEVELOPMENT
Waterloo, Ontario

A new urban core has been designed to form a vital city centre on a vacant 12-acre industrial site devastated by fire. Two 19th century barrel storage warehouses are to be transformed into civic buildings that front onto a new public square.

TORONTO HISTORICAL BOARD OFFICES
Toronto, Ontario

The former Bank of Toronto, designed in 1905 by E.J. Lennox, was renovated and restored to serve as headquarters of the Toronto Historical Board. The restoration was faithful to the intentions of the original design without compromising contemporary usefulness.

CIBC LEADERSHIP
DEVELOPMENT CENTRE
King City, Ontario

A spa and hotel, originally designed by
Arthur Erickson, were transformed to
provide a national learning centre for
employees of the Canadian Imperial
Bank of Commerce. An indoor tennis
court was converted to an auditorium
with retractable raked seating for 300.
Exercise rooms became multi-media
classrooms and the spa converted to a
computer-assisted decision support
centre for executive training.

GEORGE DUNBAR BRIDGE
Ottawa, Ontario
(with McCormick Rankin
Engineers Ltd.)

Engineering and civic design were key
factors in the design of a bridge for a
highway linking the airport to the city
centre. The scale of the supporting structure, the arc of its trusses, and the
deployment of regular lookout points
and lighting were used to give rhythm
and appropriate scale to an otherwise
utilitarian element in the landscape.

HAMILTON CITY HALL
GROUNDS PLAN
Hamilton, Ontario

The grounds plan includes not only a
new plaza for public gatherings and
entry to City Hall but also proposes a
memorial grove with commemorative
sculptures on new terraces planted
with sycamore trees. The landscape
provides a context and foil for the
modern architecture of the existing
freestanding City Hall.

IMPERIAL THEATRE
St. John, New Brunswick
(with MMC Architects Ltd.)

An ornate vaudeville theatre, circa 1913,
was renovated to provide the city with a
performing arts facility. The work included rebuilding the stage, modifying
the proscenium arch, adding an orches-
tra pit, changing the rake of seating and
redesigning the lobbies.

NORTH CAMPUS
ATHLETIC FACILITY
University of Waterloo
Waterloo, Ontario

An addition to an existing ice arena, the
facility includes a new gymnasium and
fitness rooms, the headquarters for the
campus football team, and locker,
therapy and meeting rooms.

**GEORGE BROWN COLLEGE
RENOVATIONS**
Toronto, Ontario
(Phase 1 with Craig Dubbledam
Architect Ltd.)

The College embarked on an ambitious
program to consolidate four campuses
into two in order to reduce operating
costs, reorganize academic space for
greater effectiveness, and provide
adequate mechanical and electrical support for teaching and computer uses.
The redesign has materially improved
the quality of facilities for teaching,
faculty and students.

**HUIYANG GOLF AND
COUNTRY CLUB**
People's Republic of China
(with SRT Architects Ltd.)

The master plan for an integrated resort
was designed to include a country club,
dining and support facilities and living
areas. A variety of single-family houses,
townhouses, lowrise apartments, and
two hotels, each with 200 rooms, are
grouped around a 72 par championship
golf course.

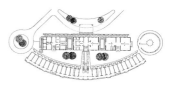

MISSISSAUGA TRANSIT TERMINAL
Mississauga, Ontario
(with McCormick Rankin
Engineers Ltd.)

This three-level terminal provides a nat-
urally lit and climate-controlled station
for passengers. Natural lighting is introduced via clerestory windows and an
open well penetrating to the lowest
level. The lowest level is a pedestrian
concourse that connects the terminal to
a regional shopping centre.

NEW WORLD GARDENS
Dongguan, People's Republic of China
(with SRT Architects Ltd.)

A community plan provides for the
phased development of housing for
12,000 people. The plan includes a
large man-made lake, shopping
precinct, schools and a community
centre, with detailed design of 18
different housing types.

RESIDENTIAL DEVELOPMENT
Beijing, People's Republic of China
(with SRT Architects Ltd.)

Three residential enclaves are located at
the edge of a civic park. Each enclave
incorporates a mix of townhouses and
detached houses ranging in size from
200 to 400 square metres.

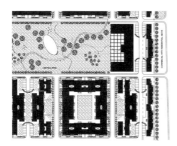

1994

AGNES ETHERINGTON ART CENTRE COMPETITION
Queen's University
Kingston, Ontario
(with Shoalts and Zaback Architects Ltd.)

The competition design incorporates an art museum to house the Bader Collection of Renaissance paintings, a conservation school, library, auditorium and faculty offices. Included in the design is the restoration of a 19th century house and garden, and a new sculpture plaza and cloister to serve the broader university community.

ARCHIVES OF ONTARIO
Toronto, Ontario

The design provides for an expanded and publicly visible provincial archives within a restored Ontario government building on the Canadian National Exhibition grounds. The existing building was adapted to accommodate an expanded public exhibition and interpretative program. A new wing was designed to house the archives in conditions of strict environmental control and security.

BALLET/OPERA HOUSE
Toronto, Ontario

The Canadian Opera Company and the adjacent Canadian Stage Company occupy a block of 19th century buildings that once housed the Toronto Gas Company. The design demonstrates the feasibility of accommodating a new ballet/opera theatre with four stages while maintaining rehearsal support and administrative offices within the site occupied by the existing historic buildings.

BALMORAL APARTMENTS
Toronto, Ontario

Located near a major intersection, a subway stop and parkland, the design reinforces the use and density pattern of the Toronto superblock system. The largest component, an eight-storey building, lies along an arterial street. Shops occupy the ground level. The wings of the building are stepped, culminating in townhouses which align with adjacent housing.

BURLINGTON DOWNTOWN WATERFRONT EAST MASTER PLAN
Burlington, Ontario

The creation of offshore islands will provide storm protection and wildlife habitats, and allow construction of this mixed-use project at the edge of Lake Ontario. The complex consists of two apartment buildings, an office building, a community theatre, parking, one indoor and three outdoor public squares. With this development, the extension of the city's street grid, and the construction of a waterfront promenade, the city will gain renewed access to the lakefront.

ONTARIO LEGISLATURE BUILDING INTERIOR RENOVATION AND RESTORATION
Toronto, Ontario

The provincial parliament building and its grounds, dating from 1893, are in need of comprehensive renovation. New mechanical, electrical, communications and safety systems are being introduced, and interior spaces and finishes are being restored.

121

VISITOR ORIENTATION CENTRE
Ottawa, Ontario
(with Katz Webster Clancy
Architects Ltd)

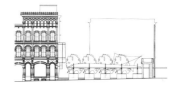

At this site on Wellington Street,
directly opposite the federal parliament
buildings, visitors are provided with
information and interpretation of the
national capital region. The centre consists of a public square, exhibition space
and multimedia theatre.

1995

**BAYCREST JEWISH CENTRE
FOR GERIATRIC CARE**
North York, Ontario
(with Boigon, Petroff, Shepherd
Architects Inc.)

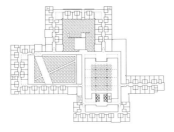

The centre includes a 372-bed long-
term care facility and a 100-bed centre
for cognitive disorders. The design
provides for clusters of private rooms
with common living and dining
areas and easy access to the outdoors,
in order to create a home-like
environment.

CN LANDS DEVELOPMENT
Sarnia, Ontario

Former industrial lands have been
planned to accommodate leisure,
recreation and commercial uses, and
restore access to the waterfront. The
first phase of development will be an
ice arena, exhibition hall and indoor
swimming pool.

**CENTRE FOR ENVIRONMENTAL
STUDIES AND ENGINEERING
COMPETITION**
University of Waterloo
Waterloo, Ontario
(with Snider Reichard March
Architects Ltd.)

The design provides effective laboratory
and faculty office space, consolidates and
provides coherent focus to new and existing facilities, and reintegrates the site with
the campus. A traditional college quadrangle was integral to the design solution.

CORNWALL CENTRAL LIBRARY
Cornwall, Ontario
(with Shoalts and Zaback
Architects Ltd.)

A large post office and mail distribution
terminal dating from 1953 is being transformed into the main library for the city.
The design accommodates the latest information technology and makes provision
for library flexibility and user comfort.

CREATIVE ARTS FACILITY

University of British Columbia
Vancouver, British Columbia
(with Tielker Sim Harrison Weller
Architects Ltd.)

The building houses the departments
of music, drama, fine arts and film,
and provides a link in the university
pedestrian system. The walk on the
long frontage of the building defines
the edge of the West Mall and provides
access to studios, the service court
and the arts quadrangle.

DIAMOND MOUNTAIN VINEYARD

Calistoga, California

A house for the vineyard owner is
situated on the brow of Diamond
Mountain, overlooking the Napa Valley.
The elongated building is designed to
minimize its impact on the vineyard,
provide privacy from the approach road
and openness to the view.

ETOBICOKE MEMORIAL POOL/
OUR LADY OF SORROWS
ELEMENTARY SCHOOL

Etobicoke, Ontario
(with G. Bruce Stratton Architect)

A new public pool and school will join
an existing indoor ice arena at the edge
of a park system along Mimico Creek
to form a community centre for the
neighbourhood. The design provides
for uses to be shared by the separate
institutions while maintaining their
separate identities.

FOREIGN MINISTRY COMPETITION

Jerusalem, Israel
(with Kolker Kolker Epstein Architects)

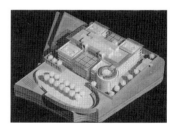

The plan for this invited anonymous
design competition is designed to meet
the particular requirements of the for-
eign ministry of Israel. The building is
also intended to be a prototype of office
design in a Middle Eastern context.

GARLAND RESIDENCE

Toronto, Ontario

The house is designed for a ravine site
in Rosedale. Its mass has been shaped to
maintain unobstructed views of the historic house to the east, and to mediate
between the continuous streetscape to
the west and the open space surrounding the historic house. The main floor is
a continuous series of living spaces,
with bedrooms and library above.

IBM CANADA OFFICE
BUILDING RENOVATION

Markham, Ontario

The particular configuration of public
space and security requirements of a
large office facility, originally built for
IBM, are being modified to accommodate multiple tenancy.

JERUSALEM GATEWAY
Jerusalem, Israel
(with Kolker Kolker Epstein Architects)

This mixed-use project consists of a 10,000-seat multipurpose stadium, a new intercity bus terminal at a key transportation hub, 900 hotel rooms, 3500 square meters of retail space, parking for 3600 cars and associated public open spaces. The stadium and exhibition space will have a direct connection to the adjacent international convention centre.

JEWISH COMMUNITY CENTRE FOR THE UPPER WEST SIDE
New York City, New York

This centre will provide athletic, social, cultural and educational programs for a full spectrum of users, from infants to the elderly. Situated at the corner of Amsterdam Avenue and 76th Street, it will be the physical and symbolic centre of this Manhattan community.

LAW SCHOOL RENOVATION MASTER PLAN
Queen's University
Kingston, Ontario

The law school has grown in an ad hoc manner, with a diverse collection of linked buildings. The new plan accommodates the law program in appropriate spaces and locations, incorporates the use of natural light, and provides comfortable and accessible facilities for the users.

ONTARIO MINISTRY OF LABOUR OFFICES
Toronto, Ontario

The renovation involves a complete refit of 170,000 square feet on 12 floors within an existing office tower. The new offices will accommodate 650 people. Although half of the work area consists of enclosed offices, the building perimeter is kept free of visual obstructions to permit natural light and external views.

OTONABEE COLLEGE RENOVATION TRENT UNIVERSITY
Peterborough, Ontario
(with Johan de Villiers Architect)

This retrofit of an existing university building is innovative in two ways. The building shell is designed to act as a dynamic buffer zone. Air is circulated within a double membrane, mediating between exterior and interior temperatures. In addition, "breathing wall" technology is incorporated to improve air quality.

PROSPECT CEMETERY MAUSOLEUM
Toronto, Ontario

The mausoleum accommodates 750 crypts in a series of pavilions, exterior courts and a tower. The exterior is clad in split-face granite, and the interiors in polished marble.

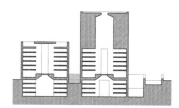

ST. MICHAEL'S HOSPITAL
MASTER PLAN
Toronto, Ontario

The master plan charts the reorganiza-
tion and expansion of the hospital to
the year 2015. Ability to accommodate
changes in the organization of health
care delivery and constantly improving
medical technology were important
factors in planning the hospital.
Implementation of the plan will also
improve the existing buildings and
their services.

SCHOOL OF JOURNALISM
UNIVERSITY OF BRITISH COLUMBIA
Vancouver, British Columbia
(with Tielker Sim Harrison
Weller Architects Ltd.)

This new three-storey structure is an
anchor to the Creative Arts Facility
building and quadrangle. Seminar
rooms and faculty offices are designed
to capture the long view towards Howe
Sound and the Pacific Ocean.

SOUTH RIVERDALE
COMMUNITY HEALTH CENTRE
Toronto, Ontario

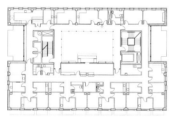

The centre is a new building on a
neighbourhood main street, providing
primary health care, family planning,
social services and health promotion.
The health centre is a community-
operated organization and is part of a
provincial government plan to decen-
tralize health care.

SOUTHEAST BRANCH LIBRARY
York, Ontario

Situated on the corner of a local main
street, the branch library serves its
immediate neighbourhood. In addition
to the collection, reading areas and
access to information technology, the
library houses an arts centre and a
150-seat theatre.

YONGE AND STEELES
URBAN PRECINCT MASTER PLAN
Markham, Ontario

The plan sets out guidelines to shape
building form and public open space at
a major road intersection. The guidelines propose reinforcement of the
existing street and block structure,
graduating building height from its
highest level on Yonge Street down to
height and building setbacks consistent
with the existing single-family
neighbourhood to the east.

All photographs by Steven Evans except where noted.

A DEFINITION OF ARCHITECTURE

BY A.J. DIAMOND

Too often architecture is defined as an art or as a science, as a subjective reaction to circumstance or as an objective analysis – or is viewed exclusively in some other aesthetic, technological or social terms. It is none of these aspects alone, but all of them in varying degrees. Most significantly, architecture is distinguished by its primary purpose – the accommodation of human activity. Therefore, it can never be seen in a purely abstract way, nor in a purely technological one. It is neither pure sculpture nor machine. It is architecture.

What identifies mature and gratifying works of architecture is the breadth of consideration and the judgment about which aspects in any particular instance are given emphasis.

An inclusive analysis should consider social, technical, political, financial, environmental, physical and symbolic factors. It is better to attempt to address all aspects of the design problem than to succeed spectacularly in one. There are circumstances which call for buildings which stand out. Such circumstances are rare, however, if the broader question of the consequences on the aggregate environment are considered. Most circumstances call for buildings which, instead of drawing attention to themselves, fit their context as a small increment of a harmonious whole.

It follows that "design" should not be an end in itself. Thus the general issue of ends and means should be raised, and also the relationship between style and content. Those two issues are closely related.

When means become ends themselves, style is divorced from content and becomes mere packaging. But ends, defined by both content and context, are realized by appropriate means. The results can be tested objectively rather than subjectively, and thus rational discourse about success or failure can take place. By this type of objective analysis, architectural criticism can also be distinguished from the esoterica of aesthetic judgment.

None of this is to say that design that transcends the primary purposes of sheltering and facilitating human activity cannot or should not occur. Indeed, the greatest architecture is elevated in precisely this way. But this is not accomplished at the expense of its primary purposes. The sublime assimilation of purpose, technique and architectonic facility marks just such work as distinguished.

Given that space and its social purposes is the metier of architecture, it is well to understand how this central medium has been treated by architects over time, and how they attempt to complete the integration of space, function and construction technique. Of course technique, in the technological sense, has not always been important. While technology or craft was of prime importance to the Comacine, the stone masons who built the Gothic cathedrals of Europe, the same was not true of the artist-architects of the Italian Renaissance. However, the principles which underlie spatial organization can be discerned in every period of building, regardless of architectural language.

At one end of the spectrum is the principle of classical enclosure. Here the definition of space and its enclosure is very clear. Walls, floors, ceilings are finite and intersect with precision. Apertures, whether doors or windows, are equally well defined. Thus passage from without to within is unmistakable. The other end of this spectrum is represented in its most extreme form by the modern or international movement of the early 20th century, and perhaps one could argue was introduced originally by baroque architecture. Gideon, in *Space, Time and Architecture*, described this form of spatial organiztion as the "interpenetration of space." Continuity, transparency and the lack of precise definition of enclosure characterizes this form of spatial organization. In baroque forms, floor, wall and ceiling planes do not meet with precision. In modern architecture, passage from without to within is deliberately obscure, as is the threshold between spaces.

Just as the balance or resolution of extremes often characterizes the most gratifying work in literature, painting, sculpture or music, so it is also in architecture and its essential element, space. Therefore an essential component of a critical review of the projects illustrated here – and most notably the Metro-Central YMCA, the York University Student Centre and the Richmond Hill Central Library – must be the success or failure of the attempt to resolve the extremes of spatial organization.

As mentioned before, in evaluating architecture at least two other factors must be considered – the social or human purposes for which the building is intended, and the degree to which the abstractions of spatial organization and the social intentions have been served by technology.

In viewing the YMCA, the York Student Centre and the Richmond Hill Library, the program can generally be read on the exterior, in terms of both function and space. Both room definition and transparency occur. Room or space definition is not only given by walls in a conventional manner, but also inferred by the placement of structural elements and the integration between mechanical systems and structure.

Context must also be taken into account when judging buildings. In a sense, the previous factors discussed exert centrifugal pressure as a result of designing from the inside out. An equally important pressure, that of contextual considerations, exerts centripetal force. Questions of scale are central in this regard. Two of the three buildings cited deal most particularly with this broad issue. The student centre and the library both face large open spaces. Thus, elements capable of imparting a scale commensurate with their large scale settings have been employed. A monolithic piano nobile, columns two storeys in height that unite the two floors of student offices, and substantial roof eaves provide such large scale components in the student centre. In the design of the library, the structural piers have been carried from ground to roof, and contrast in colour, tone and texture with the glazing and spandrels between. Only in close proximity do the design details of the panels, and their smaller scale elements, appropriately reveal themselves. The symbolic importance of the library as a public institution is also reflected in the monumentality that such scale represents. Clear transference of weight, that is accepting gravitational force, is another way in which permanence can be conveyed, reflective of an enduring institution.

By handling the elements of a building in a manner that satisfies more than their primary purposes, architecture can be elevated above building. For example, columns might not only carry building loads but define space, moderate light and give scale. Mechanical systems may not only deliver power or ventilation but also give rhythm and proportion to space. Lighting can serve not only to illuminate but also to emphasize and give character to place.

While the primary purpose of buildings is to accommodate human activity, architeture, like literature, the fine arts, music and film, can be viewed at many levels – pictorial, narrative, emotional, literal, metaphysical and political. What characterizes the best architecture is inclusiveness and the enrichment it can provide to individuals and to society as a whole.

AWARDS

1969

YORK SQUARE
Ontario Association of Architects
Award of Excellence

Habitation Space International Award

1971

ALCAN PRODUCTS HEAD OFFICE
(TORONTO, ONTARIO)
Aluminum Company of Canada
Annual Design Award

Ontario Association of Architects
Award of Excellence

ONTARIO MEDICAL ASSOCIATION
Ontario Masons' Relations Council
Award of Excellence

Ontario Medical Association
Award of Merit

1972

ONTARIO MEDICAL ASSOCIATION
Canadian Design Council
Masonry Award

YORK SQUARE
Canadian Design Council
Masonry Award

Design Canada
Merit Citation

1974

DIAMOND AND MYERS
Toronto Historical Board
Award of Merit for contribution
to historical preservation

HOUSING UNION BUILDING
UNIVERSITY OF ALBERTA
Canadian Housing Design Council
Award for Residential Design
Honorable Mention

1975

DUNDAS-SHERBOURNE HOUSING	Heritage Canada National Honour Award
HOUSING UNION BUILDING	Stelco Corporation Design in Steel Award
	The Canadian Mortgage and Housing Corporation Award for Residential Design Honorable Mention

1976

DUNDAS-SHERBOURNE HOUSING	City of Toronto Non-Profit Housing Corporation Award
	Ontario Association of Architects Award of Excellence
BEVERLEY PLACE (HYDRO BLOCK)	City of Toronto Non-Profit Housing Corporation Neighbourhood Development Award
	Urban Design Magazine Award

1977

STUDENT HOUSING QUEEN'S UNIVERSITY	Heritage Canada Regional Award of Honour
TALKA COMMUNITY	*Canadian Architect* Magazine Yearbook Award of Excellence

1978

CITADEL THEATRE	Stelco Design Award
	City of Edmonton Design Award
DUNDAS-SHERBOURNE HOUSING	Canadian Housing Design Council Award
	Habitation Space International Award
	Urban Design Magazine Award
WESTOVER PARK ESTATES	*Canadian Architect* Magazine Yearbook Award of Excellence

1979

A.J. DIAMOND   Heritage Canada
                                          Communications Award

1982

ALCAN ALUMINUM CORPORATION LTD.   *Interiors* Magazine
(CLEVELAND, OHIO)   Fourth Annual Interiors Award

METRO-CENTRAL YMCA   *Canadian Architect* Magazine
                                          Award of Excellence

1983

BERKELEY CASTLE   Credit Foncier Award
                                          Honorable Mention

ELIZABETH CHESTNUT APARTMENTS   *Canadian Architect* Magazine
                                          Award of Excellence

VILLAGE TERRACE   Ontario Association of Architects
                                          Residential Award
                                          Award of Excellence

                                          Ontario Masons' Relations Council
                                          Award of Excellence

1984

BERKELEY CASTLE   Heritage Canada Foundation
                                          National Award of Honour

                                          Ontario Masons' Relations Council
                                          Award of Excellence

JAPAN RESTAURANT CENTRE   *Canadian Architect* Magazine
                                          Award of Excellence

1985

METRO-CENTRAL YMCA   Ontario Masons' Relations Council
                                          Award of Excellence

VILLAGE TERRACE   Canadian Housing Design
                                          Council Award

                                          Governor-General's Award
                                          for Architecture

1986

BURNS BUILDING	Credit Foncier Award
CITADEL THEATRE	Governor-General's Award for Architecture
METRO-CENTRAL YMCA	Governor-General's Medal for Architecture

1987

METRO-CENTRAL YMCA	Ontario Association of Architects Design Award

1988

OLYMPIC ARCH	1988 Calgary Olympics Arts Festival Gold Medal

1989

A.J. DIAMOND	City of Toronto Toronto Arts Award for Architecture and Design
NATIONAL BALLET SCHOOL	Toronto Historical Board Award of Merit
YORK UNIVERSITY STUDENT CENTRE	*Canadian Architect* Magazine Award of Excellence

1990

BURNS HALL OFFICERS' TRAINING FACILITY	City of North York Design Award
EARTH SCIENCES CENTRE UNIVERSITY OF TORONTO	Ontario Masons' Relations Council Award of Excellence
	Toronto Historical Board Award of Merit
JERUSALEM CITY HALL	*Canadian Architect* Magazine Award of Excellence

1991

BURNS HALL OFFICERS' TRAINING FACILITY	Ontario Masons' Relations Council Honorable Mention

1991 *cont'd*

JERUSALEM CITY HALL	ARRIS Computer Design Award
LOIS HANCEY AQUATIC CENTRE	ARRIS Computer Design Award
NEWCASTLE TOWN HALL	Ontario Association of Architects Award of Excellence
QUEEN'S UNIVERSITY LIBRARY	ARRIS Computer Design Award
RICHMOND HILL CENTRAL LIBRARY	ARRIS Computer Design Award

1992

BURLINGTON HOUSING INTENSIFICATION STUDY	Ontario Professional Planners Institute Award of Excellence – Communication
YORK SQUARE	City of Toronto 25-Year *Urban Design* Award
YORK UNIVERSITY STUDENT CENTRE	Ontario Masons Relations Council Award of Excellence

1993

YORK UNIVERSITY STUDENT CENTRE	Portland Cement Association Concrete Building Award
	City of North York Design Award

1994

A.J. DIAMOND FOR JERUSALEM CITY HALL	The American Society of Architectural Perspectivist Award
EARTH SCIENCES CENTRE UNIVERSITY OF TORONTO	Governor-General's Award for Architecture
RICHMOND HILL CENTRAL LIBRARY	Governor-General's Award for Architecture
	Portland Cement Association Concrete Building Award

1995

EARTH SCIENCES CENTRE UNIVERSITY OF TORONTO	City of Toronto *Urban Design* Award
RICHMOND HILL CENTRAL LIBRARY	Financial Post Design Effectiveness Awards for Architectural Design

SELECTED BIBLIOGRAPHY

WRITINGS BY A.J. DIAMOND

1963. "Participant's-Eye Views 1: Seminar at Cranbrook." *Journal of Architectural Education* 18(3), December: 38-39.

1965-70. Architecture Canada (Royal Architectural Institute of Canada). (Associate/Contributing Editor during these years).

1966. "Universities, Introduction." *Architecture Canada* 43(10), October: 43.

1967. "The New City." *Habitat* 10(1), January/February: 33-35.

1967. "Expo 67." *AIA Journal (American Institute of Architects)* 47(2), February: 42-56.

1967. "Expo and the Future City." *Parallel* 1(6), February/March: 32-36.

1968. "A Plea for Performance Standards." *AIA Journal (American Institute of Architects)* 50(1), July: 54-55.

1969. "Design Priorities Questioned." *Architecture Canada* (9), September: 14.

1971. "Two Aspects of Services – Quality and Economy." *Canadian Building,* September: 28.

1972. "Density, Distribution and Costs." Research paper for Central Mortage and Housing Corporation.

1974. "Town Building or Town Planning?" *Canadian Architect* 19(1), January: 35-36.

1976. "Residential Density and Housing Form." *Journal of Architectural Education* 29(3), February: 15-16.

1978. "On Sleeping With an Elephant: Canada and America." *Process: Architecture* 5: 26-29.

1978. "P.O.V.: What this Country Needs is a Good Provincial Architecture." *Toronto Life,* May: 190.

1978. "A Sense of Place." *Canadian Forum* 58(681): June/July: 10-11.

1979. "Rehabilitation in Practice." In *Rehabilitation of Buildings: Proceedings* (Second Canadian Building Congress, Toronto, Ontario. October 15-17, 1979). Ottawa: National Research Council of Canada. Pages 15-22.

1981. "Renovation Design." *LCN Newsletter,* April: 1-4.

1982. "A Critique of the Planning and Building Design of Winnipeg." In *The Winter City* (Conference sponsored by the Canadian Housing Design Council in co-operation with the Continuing Education Division, the University of Manitoba, Winter 1982). Winnipeg: Canadian Housing Design Council. Pages 3-8.

1992. "Staying in Shape." *Toronto Life,* November: 56-59.

1995. "Die Kosten trägt die Allgemeinheit: Über Einkaufszentren auf der grünen Wiese." *planen + bauen,* June: 27.

1980. "Urban Consolidation and Infill." *LCN Newsletter,* June: 1-4.

1987. "Western Section – Bathurst Street to Humber River." In *A Charette in the City: The Gardiner Expressway* (O.A.A. Convention, Toronto, March 4-6, 1987). Toronto: Ontario Association of Architects. Pages 29-43.

1987. "O.A.A. Charette, A Report: Team Three, Western Section." *Canadian Architect* 32(7), July: 36-37.

1987. "Consensus and Other Concerns." *Canadian Architect* 32(9), September: 18-33. (Editor).

1990. *Housing on Toronto's Main Streets: A Design Competition: Conditions and Programme.* Toronto: City of Toronto.

1993. "Case Studies: Critique." In *Public Art Symposium: Report of the Proceedings* (Mayor's Symposium on Public Art, Hamilton, Ontario, May 30, 1992). Edited by Cheryl York. Hamilton: Department of Culture and Recreation, City of Hamilton. Pages 31-39.

ABOUT THE FIRM AND CONTEMPORARY ARCHITECTURAL ISSUES

1968. Mitchell, Harris. "Small Change, Big Improvement." *Canadian Homes,* August: 6-9.

1972. "A.J. Diamond and Barton Myers: 15 Works." *a + u (Architecture & Urbanism)* 2(5), May: 15-63.

1973. "Cities: the Low-rise Alternative." *Time,* 16 April: 14-16.

1975. Kuwabara, Bruce and Barry Sampson. "Diamond and Myers: The Form of Reform/Great Canadian Architects and Planners 3." *City Magazine* 1(5/6), August/September: 29-47.

1976. "Jack Diamond." *Heritage Canada* 2(3), Summer: 39.

1978. Jackson, Anthony. *The Democratization of Canadian Architecture* (Library of Canadian Architecture). Halifax: Tech-Press.

1978. "House: Toronto, Ontario, Canada – Architect: Jack Diamond." *a + u (Architecture & Urbanism)* 78(96), September: 177-84.

1979. Littman, Sol. "Jack Diamond's Architecture Has Changed Toronto's Face." *Toronto Star,* 4 March.

1979. "The Communication Awards." *Heritage Canada* 5(4), October: 24-25.

1979. McKelvey, Merilyn. "Main Street and Heritage Conservation." *LCN Newsletter,* October: 1-6.

1980. "Can Our Downtowns Be Saved?" *Canadian Heritage,* April: 46-48.

1981. Bernstein, William and Ruth Cawker. *Contemporary Canadian Architecture: The Mainstream and Beyond.* Don Mills, Ontario: Fitzhenry and Whiteside.

1981. Cawker, Ruth and William Bernstein (Compilers). *Building with Words: Canadian Architects on Architecture.* Toronto: Coach House Press.

1981. Garland, Kevin and Paul Syme. "Conversion and Renovation for Residential Use." *LCN Newsletter,* November: 1-6.

1982. Stacey, Robert (Editor). *OKanada.* Ottawa: Canada Council. Exhibition Catalogue.

1982. Garland, Kevin. "Infill Downtown." *CIP Forum ICU* 1(Special Issue), February: 9-10.

1982. Royle, John C. "Sprawl, the Curse of North America." *Community Ontario* 26(2), March/April: 12-13.

1983. "From Mies to Metaphors." *Canadian Architect* 28(5), May: 23-38.

ABOUT THE FIRM AND CONTEMPORARY ARCHITECTURAL ISSUES *cont'd*

1984. *Architecture Overseas: An RIBA Festival of Architecture Exhibition.* London: UIA-International Architect Magazine. Pages 40-43.

1984. Boone, Ned. "The Box Rebellion." *Homes* (Toronto Life), Spring: H47-48.

1985. Simmins, Geoffrey. "Jack Diamond." *City and Country Home* 4(7), November: 129-38.

1986. Boddy, Trevor. "Making/Breaking the Canadian Street." In *Metropolitan Mutations: The Architecture of Emerging Public Spaces* (R.A.I.C. Annual: 1). Edited by Detlef Mertins. Toronto: Little, Brown and Company (Canada) Limited. Pages 167-78.

1986. *The Interpretation of Architecture* (Exhibition curated by Janice Gurney and others). Toronto: YYZ Gallery. Exhibition catalogue.

1986. Ontario Ministry of Citizenship and Culture. *Building Libraries: Guidelines for the Planning and Design of Ontario Public Libraries.* Toronto: The Ministry.

1987. Boddy, Trevor. "The Bush League: Four Approaches to Regionalism in Recent Canadian Architecture." *Center: A Journal for Architecture in America* 3: 100-107.

1987. Robinson, John. "Donald Schmitt: Architecture for People." *Toronto Star,* 26 April: E1-4.

1987. Lasker, David. "The Charette." *Perspectives (The Newsletter of the Ontario Association of Architects)* 1(1), July: 2-5.

1987. Simmins, Geoffrey. "The Diamond Setting." *City and Country Home,* November 6(9): 96-105.

1988. Cawker, Ruth and William Bernstein. *Contemporary Canadian Architecture: The Mainstream and Beyond.* Revised and Expanded Edition. Markham, Ontario: Fitzhenry and Whiteside.

1988. Nelson, Trudie. "Shoebox Grandeur." *Chatelaine,* February: 64-67.

1989. Freedman, Adele. "Design for Dining." *Canadian Art* 6(2), Summer: 68-72.

1989. *Toronto Arts Awards: Official Program.* (October 12, 1989).

1990. Falconer, Tim. "Diamond Mined." *Toronto Life,* March: 90-96.

1991. "CAD on the IBM and Workstation." *Contract* 10(1), February/March: 34-40.

1991. "Housing on Toronto's Main Streets". *Places: A Quarterly Journal of Environmental Design* 7(2), Winter: 48-76.

1992. *Architecture in Perspective 7: A Competitive Exhibition of Architectural Delineation.* Boston: American Society of Architectural Perspectivists.

1992. *Callwood's National Treasures: Jack Diamond* (Interview with June Callwood, May 20, 1992). Toronto: Produced by Contact Communications for VISION TV. Videotape.

1992. *New Directions in Ontario Architecture: A Juried Exhibition of Buildings 1989-1991.* Don Mills, Ontario: Ontario Association of Architects.

1992. Crinion, Elizabeth. "The Right Angles." *Canadian House & Home* 14(1), February/March: 48-53.

1992. Rybczynski, Witold. "Diamond's Style Forever." *Globe and Mail,* 9 June: D10.

1992. Rochon, Lisa. "Human Designs." *International Contract,* June/July: 3 pages.

1993. *Adrienne Clarkson Presents: A.J. Diamond – Architect.* Toronto: Canadian Broadcasting Corporation. Videotape.

1993. Godfrey, Stephen. "On to the High-tech Drawing Board: Concrete Castles in the Air." *Globe and Mail (Arts Weekend),* 9 January: C1.

1993. Ferrara, Luigi. "Going Global: Ontario Architects Take the Leap." *Perspectives (The Journal of the Ontario Association of Architects)* 1(1), Spring: 8-13.

1993. Ashdown, Ian. "Virtual Photometry." *Lighting Design + Application* 23(12), December: 33-39.

1994. Emanuel, Muriel (Editor). *Contemporary Architects.* 3rd Edition. New York: St. Martin's Press.

1994. Kalman, Harold. *A History of Canadian Architecture: Volume 2.* Toronto: Oxford University Press.

1994. Gzowski, Peter. "Windows and Rooms: Peter Gzowski Interviews A.J. Diamond." *Brick* (48), Spring: 46-58.

1994. Mahoney, Diana Phillips. "Walking Through Architectural Designs." *Computer Graphics World* 17(6), June: 22-30.

1995. Warson, Albert. "Altered States: Canada." *World Architecture* (37): 65-67.

ABOUT SPECIFIC PROJECTS AND COMPETITIONS

ONTARIO MEDICAL ASSOCIATION, TORONTO, ONTARIO

1971. "Office for Ontario Medical Association, Toronto." *Canadian Architect* 16(6), June: 30-35.

1971. "Common Parts and Legible Spaces in Toronto's O.M.A. Building." *Architectural Record* 150(3), September: 127-34.

1980. "Ontario Medical Association." *Architectural Review* 167(999), May: 295.

YORK SQUARE, TORONTO, ONTARIO

1969. "York Square, Toronto." *Canadian Architect* 14(6), June: 36-38.

1969. "Urban Supertoy Subdues Renewal Bulldozer." *Progressive Architecture* 50(9), September: 144-53.

1969. "York Square." *Byggekunst,* September: 53.

1971. "Integrierte Grafik." *Moebel Interior Design* 3: 38-43.

1971. "A Sculptural Stair Rising Through Curved Space Turns This Old House on Toronto's Lively York Square Into a Glamorous, Spacious Environment for Haute Coiffure." *Architectural Record* 150(2), August: 96-97.

1972. "York Square Shopping Centre in Toronto." *Baumeister* 69(10), October: 1098-1101.

1983. Zeidler, Eberhard H. *Multifunktionale Architektur / Multi-Use Architecture.* New York: Van Nostrand Reinhold. Pages 36-37.

1986. Dendy, William and William Kilbourn. *Toronto Observed: Its Architecture, Patrons and History.* Toronto: Oxford University Press. Pages 297-98.

ALCAN PRODUCTS HEAD OFFICE, TORONTO, ONTARIO

1971. "Interior for Alcan: Alcan Canada Products, Toronto-Dominion Centre, Toronto." *Canadian Architect* 16(3), March: 30-35.

1972. "Alcan's Toronto Offices Sparkle with Aluminum and Light." *Architectural Record* 151(3), March: 93-96.

1972. "Three Toronto Surprises by Diamond and Myers." *Interiors* 132(3), October: 118-23.

ABOUT SPECIFIC PROJECTS AND COMPETITIONS *cont'd*

HOUSING UNION BUILDING, UNIVERSITY OF ALBERTA, EDMONTON, ALBERTA

1969. "University of Alberta: Long Range Development Plan." *Architecture Canada* 46(7/8), July/August: 37-39.

1970. "Housing on a Mall Proposed for University of Alberta Students." Architecture *Canada Magazine* 47, 13 April: 6-7.

1972. "University of Alberta and Its Student Union Building, Edmonton, Canada." *a + u (Architecture & Urbanism)* 2(5), May: 50-55.

1972. "The Campus as a Lesson in Urban Form." *Progressive Architecture* 53(9), September: 112-15.

1974. Dixon, J.M. "Students' Union Housing, University of Alberta." *Progressive Architecture* 55(2), February: 46-51.

1974. "Per 964 Studenti in Canada." *Domus* (539), October: 25-29.

1974. "Students' Union Housing, University of Alberta." *a + u (Architecture & Urbanism)* (48), December: 59-72.

1975. "Studentenwohnheim, Edmonton, CAN." *Baumeister* 72(2), February: 102-106.

1975. Franck, Claude. "La Forme Dicte la Fonction." *L'Architecture d'Aujourdhui* (179), May/June: 87-92.

1976. "University of Alberta, Student Union Housing." *Toshi-Jukatu,* Winter: 173-84.

1979. Porter, Anna and Marjorie Harris. *Farewell to the 70s.* Don Mills: Thomas Nelson. Page 221.

1980. "Barton Myers, Diamond and Myers, in Association with R.L. Wilkin: Housing Union Building (HUB), Edmonton, Alberta, Canada." *Global Architecture Document (Special Issue 1970-1980).* Pages 86-89.

1980. Scala, Alexander (Editor). *Treasures of Canada.* Toronto: Samuel-Stevens Publishers Ltd. Page 360.

1980. "Linear Atria." *Architectural Review* 167(999), May: 285.

1983. Whiteson, Leon. *Modern Canadian Architecture.* Edmonton: Hurtig Publishers. Pages 82-85.

1983. Zeidler, Eberhard H. *Multifunktionale Architektur / Multi-Use Architecture.* New York: Van Nostrand Reinhold. Pages 52-53.

1987. Boddy, Trevor. *Modern Architecture in Alberta.* Edmonton: Alberta Culture and Multiculturalism and Canadian Plains Research Centre. Pages 105-106.

1989. White, Sylvia Hart. *Sourcebook of Contemporary North American Architecture.* New York: Van Nostrand Reinhold. Pages 24-25.

CITADEL THEATRE, EDMONTON, ALBERTA

1977. "Citadel Theatre, Edmonton." *Canadian Architect* 22(7), July: 18-23.

1977. Smith, C. Ray. "Monochromatic Contextualism." *Progressive Architecture* 58(7), July: 68-71.

1977. Thom, Ron. "Citadel Theatre: Critique." *Canadian Architect* 22(7), July: 24-27.

1978. "Citadel Theatre in Edmonton, CDN." *Baumeister* (2), February: 140-143.

1978. "Canadian Citadel." *Architectural Review* 164(977), July: 6-8.

1979. "Thedel" *Informs de la Construction* (316), December: 3-15.

1980. Scala, Alexander (Editor). *Treasures of Canada.* Toronto: Samuel-Stevens Publishers Ltd. Pages 355, 358.

1980. "Citadel Theatre." *Canadian Interiors* 17(10), September/October: 44-45.

1981. Bernstein, William and Ruth Cawker. *Contemporary Canadian Architecture: The Mainstream and Beyond.* Don Mills, Ontario: Fitzhenry and Whiteside. Pages 172-79.

1983. Whiteson, Leon. *Modern Canadian Architecture.* Edmonton: Hurtig Publishers. Pages 78-81.

1984. Redstone, Louis G. *Masonry in Architecture.* New York: McGraw-Hill. Page 67.

1987. Boddy, Trevor. *Modern Architecture in Alberta.* Edmonton: Alberta Culture and Multiculturalism and Canadian Plains Research Centre. Pages 105-107.

1989. White, Sylvia Hart. *Sourcebook of Contemporary North American Architecture.* New York: Van Nostrand Reinhold. Page 89.

BEVERLEY PLACE (HYDRO BLOCK), TORONTO, ONTARIO

1978. "A Hybrid Rival to High-rises Has Character." *Globe and Mail,* 15 March: 7.

1978. "Cityhome Opens Hydro Block." *Housing Ontario* 22(2), March/April: 4-5.

1979. "In Downtown Toronto: An Innovative Medium Density Low-rise Infill Housing Development." *Domus* (598), September: 10-13.

1980. "Der 'Hydro-Block' in Toronto." *Baumeister* 77(5), May: 472-75.

1980. Godfrey, Stephen. "City Housing: Whispers of Discontent." *Globe and Mail (Fanfare),* 24 May: 1.

1980. "Hydro Block, Toronto, Ontario." *a + u (Architecture & Urbanism)* (122), November: 75-80.

1982. *New Housing in Existing Neighbourhoods: Advisory Document.* Ottawa: Canada Mortgage and Housing Corporation.

INNIS COLLEGE, UNIVERSITY OF TORONTO, TORONTO, ONTARIO

1978. "Innis College, Toronto, Ontario, 1975." *Process: Architecture* 5, 102-107.

1981. Bernstein, William and Ruth Cawker. *Contemporary Canadian Architecture: The Mainstream and Beyond.* Don Mills, Ontario: Fitzhenry and Whiteside. Pages 159-65.

1981. "Innis College in Toronto." *Baumeister* 78(8), August: 816-18.

ALCAN SMELTERS AND CHEMICALS LTD., MONTRÉAL, QUÉBEC

1980. "Alcan Corporate Headquarters, Montréal." *Canadian Architect* 25(9), September: 26-28.

1980. Doubilet, Susan. "Graceful Stylization." *Progressive Architecture* 61(12), December: 68-71.

1983. Galletta, Bruno. "Uffici a Montréal." *L'Industria delle Costruzioni* (135), January: 52-57.

ARVIDA MEDICAL CLINIC, ARVIDA, QUÉBEC

1984. "Arvida Medical Clinic." *Detail* 2(2): 26 pages. Alcan Smelters and Chemicals Ltd., Montréal, Québec.

BERKELEY CASTLE, TORONTO, ONTARIO

1982. "Perspective: Renewal." *Canadian Architect* 27(9), September: 4.

1983. "Toronto Reborn." *Canadian Heritage,* August/September: 16.

1983. Toft, Marion. "Buildings Restored to Pleasant and Useful Places." *Canadian Building,* November/December: 40-42.

1985. Shelley, Michael. "Near-Derelict Site Becomes Berkeley Castle." *Building Renovation* 2(4), August/September: 22-23.

1985. "New Products from Old Mills." *Progressive Architecture* 66(11), November: 94-99.

ABOUT SPECIFIC PROJECTS AND COMPETITIONS *cont'd*

BURNS BUILDING, CALGARY, ALBERTA

1980. "Perspective: West." *Canadian Architect* 25(12), December: 4.

1985. Zielinski, Andy. "Burns Building Gives New Look to Calgary." *Building Renovation* 2(1), February/March: 22.

ALCAN ALUMINUM CORPORATION LTD., CLEVELAND, OHIO

1982. "Office Reconstruction." *Canadian Architect* 27(11), November: 16-18.

1983. Busch, Akiko. "Executive Office Winner." *Interiors* 142(6), January: 98.

1985. "Tailored to Corporate Success." *Canadian Interiors* 22(4), April: 78-79.

METRO-CENTRAL YMCA, TORONTO, ONTARIO

1982. "Award of Excellence: Metropolitan Central YMCA, Toronto." *Canadian Architect* 27(12), December: 20-23.

1985. McBride, Eve. "The New Y: A User's Report." *Toronto Life,* January: 14.

1985. "A Toronto: La Nuova Sede YMCA." *Abitare* (233), April: 92-95.

1985. Richards, Larry. "Making a Dignified Place: The Metropolitan Central YMCA, Toronto." *Canadian Architect* 30(4), April: 24-34.

1985. MacMillan, Margaret. "Lucky Gym." *World of Interiors,* May: 142-53.

1985. Richardson, Jeff. "Controversial YMCA Highly Functional." *Canadian Building,* June: 51-53.

1986. Gruft, Andrew. *A Measure of Consensus: Canadian Architecture in Transition.* Vancouver: The University of British Columbia Fine Arts Gallery.

1986. *1986 Awards Program.* Ottawa: Royal Architectural Institute of Canada. Pages 87-90.

1986. Hénault, Odile. "A Sampling of the Nation's Far-flung Works of Quality." *Architecture* 75(9), September: 68-71.

1987. Cawker, Ruth (Editor). *Toronto: Le Nouveau, Nouveau Monde: Contemporary Architecture of Toronto.* Toronto: Government of Ontario. Pages 28-29.

1987. Robinson, John. "Donald Schmitt: Architecture for People." *Toronto Star,* 26 April: E1.

1987. Lasker, David. "An Award-Winning Project of Well-Defined Spaces and Exposed Structural Elements." *Canadian Interiors* 24(12), December: 38-41.

NATIONAL BALLET SCHOOL, TORONTO, ONTARIO

1988. Fielding, Cecelia. "Canadian National Ballet School Theatre." *Theatre Design & Technology* 23(4), Winter: 29-33.

1989. Horosko, Marian. "Betty Builds Bigger." *Dance Magazine* 63(3), March: 62-63.

1989. Beamish, Mary Anne. "The National Ballet School." *Dance in Canada* (59), Spring: 15-16.

BURNS HALL OFFICERS' TRAINING FACILITY, NORTH YORK, ONTARIO

1989. "Burns Hall, North York, Ontario: Building Design." *Canadian Architect* 34(6), June: 16-21.

ABOUT SPECIFIC PROJECTS AND COMPETITIONS *cont'd*

LA TÊTE DÉFENSE COMPETITION, PARIS, FRANCE

1983. *Tête Défense* (Concourse International d'Architecture).

1983. Toft, Marian. "Toronto Architects Are the Toast of Paris." *Canadian Building,* July/August: 52-54.

VILLAGE GATE APARTMENTS, TORONTO, ONTARIO

1984. Boone, Ned. "The Box Rebellion." *Homes (Toronto Life),* Spring: H47-48.

ROYAL OPERA HOUSE COMPETITION, COVENT GARDEN, LONDON

1984. "Garden Culture: Interview with Robin Dartington." *Architects' Journal,* 11 July: 20-25.

1984. "Cullinan Diamond Rogers: Variations on a Theme." *Architects' Journal,* 25 July: 23-45.

EARTH SCIENCES CENTRE, UNIVERSITY OF TORONTO, TORONTO, ONTARIO

1986. Boddy, Trevor. "Making/Breaking the Canadian Street." In *Metropolitan Mutations: The Architecture of Emerging Public Spaces* (R.A.I.C. Annual: 1). Edited by Detlef Mertins. Toronto: Little, Brown and Company (Canada) Limited. Pages 175-76.

1990. Arcidi, Philip. "Inquiry: Campus Infill." *Progressive Architecture* 71(4), April: 100, 107.

1990. Bisi, Lucia. "Il Centro di Scienze Naturali di Toronto." *L'ARCA 37,* April: 26-33.

1990. Boddy, Trevor. "Building Appraisal: Earth Sciences Centre, University of Toronto." *Canadian Architect* 35(5), May: 28-35.

1990. Carter, Brian. "Town and Gown." *Architects' Journal* 192(6), 8 August: 28-33.

1991. "Urban Ecology: Earth Sciences Centre." *Architectural Record* 179(2), February: 108-109.

1994. Graham, Owen (Editor). *Architecture Canada: The Governor General's Awards for Architecture, 1994.* Ottawa: Canada Council and The Royal Architectural Institute of Canada. Pages 118-124.

NEWCASTLE TOWN HALL, BOWMANVILLE, ONTARIO

1991. "Civic Centre." *Canadian Building,* May: 1 page.

1991. "Newcastle Town Hall, Bowmanville." *Perspectives (The Journal of the Ontario Association of Architects)* 5(3), June: 3.

1991. "Divide and Rule: Newcastle Town Hall, Bowmanville, Ontario." *Canadian Architect* 36(5/6), June/July: 21-25.

CANADIAN CLAY AND GLASS MUSEUM COMPETITION, WATERLOO, ONTARIO

1992. Carter, Brian (Editor). *The Canadian Clay and Glass Gallery.* Halifax: Technical University of Nova Scotia. Pages 63-72.

JERUSALEM CITY HALL, JERUSALEM, ISRAEL

1990. "Jerusalem City Hall Square." *Canadian Architect* 35(7), July: 18-23.

1990. "Award of Excellence: Jerusalem City Hall Square." *Canadian Architect* 35(12), December: 13.

1991. Benotto, Catherine. "Jerusalem City Hall Square: Landscape Unites a Municipal Campus." *Landscape Architectural Review* 12(2), May: 5-10.

ABOUT SPECIFIC PROJECTS AND COMPETITIONS *cont'd*

1991. Evans, Craig. "Global Landscape: East Meets West." *Landscape Architecture* 81(8), August: 40.

1993. *Adrienne Clarkson Presents: A.J. Diamond – Architect.* Toronto: Canadian Broadcasting Corporation. Videotape.

1993. Kroyanker, David. *The Making of City Hall Complex, Jerusalem.* Jerusalem: Ariel Publishing House.

1993. Martin, Patrick. "Diamond Creates New Jewel." *Globe and Mail,* 28 June: C1.

1994. Kroyanker, David. *Jerusalem Architecture.* New York: Vendrome Press.

1995. Kroyanker, David. "The New Design Code of Jerusalem: The Fashion of Quoting." *AI: Architecture of Israel* (21), April: 4-5,16-17.

1995. "A Tale of Two Cities." *Progressive Architecture* (5), May: 38-39.

1995. Turner, Michael. "Work Abroad 1: New Civic Foundations." *Canadian Architect* 40(6), June: 16-21.

SIMPLICITY HOUSE, MUSTIQUE, ST. VINCENT AND THE GRENADINES

1992. Evans, David. "Paradise Found." *Canadian House & Home* 14(2) April, 54-61.

1994. Drucker, Stephen. "Mustique Breezes: An Architect's Caribbean Retreat." *Architectural Digest* 51(8), August: 58-63.

YORK UNIVERSITY STUDENT CENTRE, NORTH YORK, ONTARIO

1989. "York University Student Centre, Toronto: Award of Excellence." *Canadian Architect* 34(12), December: 20-22.

1990. Beesley, Philip and Corrie Burt. "Campus Showplace." *Lighting Magazine,* October: 21-22.

1992. Mertins, Detlef. "Redefining the Spaces of Modernity." *Canadian Architect* 37(5), May: 15-23.

1993. Carter, Brian. "Campus Showpiece." *Architectural Review* 193(1155), May: 24-29.

RICHMOND HILL CENTRAL LIBRARY, RICHMOND HILL, ONTARIO

1993. Freedman, Adele. "Modern Space, Classical Form." *Globe and Mail,* 23 October: C19.

1994. Owen, Graham (Editor). Architecture Canada: *The Governor General's Awards for Architecture,* 1994. Ottawa: Canada Council and The Royal Architectural Institute of Canada. Pages 150-57.

1994. Richards, Larry Wayne. "Temple on the Fringe." *Canadian Architect* 39(2), February: 14-23.

1995. Carter, Brian. "Canadian Civitas." *Architectural Review* 197(1179), May: 68-73.

1995. Soloman, Nancy B. "Wiring the Library." *Architecture* 10 October: 118-119.

QUEEN'S UNIVERSITY LIBRARY, KINGSTON, ONTARIO

1991. Ledger, Bronwen. "Queen's University Library Competition." *Canadian Architect* 36(3), March: 33-35.

THE FIRM

Jack Diamond established his practice as A.J. Diamond Architect in 1965. Barton Myers joined the firm 1969, and from 1970 to 1975 the firm operated as Diamond and Myers. When Jack Diamond established his own firm in 1975, the name was changed to A.J. Diamond Associates.

Donald Schmitt joined the firm in 1978. In 1983 he became a partner and the company name was changed to A.J. Diamond and Partners. In 1990 the name became A.J. Diamond, Donald Schmitt and Company.

Associates in 1995 include Stewart Adams, Catherine Benotto, Greg Colucci, Mary Jane Finlayson, Michael Leckman, Thom Pratt, George Przybylski, Jon Soules and Anna Carter, Comptroller.

THE PRINCIPALS

A.J. DIAMOND

Born in South Africa, Jack Diamond received his Bachelor of Architecture, with Distinction, at the University of Capetown, where he was awarded the Thornton White Prize for design, an Italian State Bursary and the Marley Scholarship. He holds a Master's Degree in Politics, Philosophy and Economics from Oxford University, where he also earned a rugby blue, and a Master of Architecture degree from the University of Pennsylvania, where he was awarded the Graham Foundation Scholarship.

After teaching as assistant professor in the School of Architecture at the University of Pennsylvania and working in the office of Louis Kahn, he emigrated to Canada to inaugurate the Master of Architecture program at the University of Toronto. He ran the program, with the rank of associate professor, from 1964 to 1970. In 1968 he established his practice in Toronto with the design of York Square.

Jack Diamond has held the rank of full professor at York University and the University of Texas. He has taught as a visiting critic at many universities including Harvard, Princeton, the University of Pennsylvania, the University of Michigan and the University of California, Berkeley.

From 1986 to 1989 he was a commissioner of the Ontario Human Rights Commission. He was made a fellow of the Royal Architectural Institute of Canada in 1980. He received the Toronto Arts Award for Design and Architecture in 1989, was named an Honourary Fellow of the American Institute of Architects in 1994, and was awarded a Doctor of Engineering, Honoris Causa, in 1995, by the Technical University of Nova Scotia. In 1995 he was appointed to the Premier of Ontario's Task Force to review the governance, taxation and planning of the Greater Toronto Area.

DONALD SCHMITT

Donald Schmitt has practiced architecture with A.J. Diamond since 1978, becoming his partner in 1983.

He studied at the University of Toronto Schools and at the School of Architecture, University of Toronto, receiving a Bachelor of Architecture in 1978. He received the Royal Architectural Institute of Canada Medal in his thesis year.

He was sessional lecturer and Adjunct Professor at the School of Architecture, University of Toronto from 1985 to 1992, and Adjunct Professor at the School of Architecture, Technical University of Nova Scotia from 1989 to 1992.

As founding Chair of the Public Art Commission in the City of Toronto, 1986 to 1993, Mr. Schmitt has been involved in public art policy formation, the One Percent for Public Art program, and art competitions within the public realm.

In 1990 Mr. Schmitt was professional advisor to the international competition Housing on Toronto's Main Streets. He has served on public art juries, the 1992 jury for the American Society of Architectural Perspectivists, and the 1992 jury for the *Canadian Architect* Magazine Awards of Excellence. He was a finalist in the Functional Sculpture Competition sponsored by the Art Gallery of Ontario and the Markham Civic Centre Public Art Competition. In 1993 he was awarded the City of Toronto Civic Medal of Service.

PARTNERS, ASSOCIATES AND MEMBERS

(SINCE 1976)

A.J. Diamond and Donald Schmitt wish to thank members of the firm whose extraordinary efforts have contributed greatly to the firm's success.

PARTNERS
Kevin Garland
Paul Syme

ASSOCIATES
Stewart Adams
Phillip Beesley
Catherine Benotto
Anna Carter
John Chandler
Greg Colucci
Mary Jane Finlayson
George Friedman
Pat Hanson
Jim Ireland
Viktors Jaunkalns
Les Klein
Michael Leckman
Andre Lessard
Henry Lowry
Merilyn Mckelvey
David Miller
Sarah Pearce
Thom Pratt
George Przybylski
Dereck Revington
Jon Soules
Wilfrid Worland

MEMBERS
Shary Adams
Bill Anderson
Rick Andreghetti
Lynn Appleby
Cheryl Atkinson
Craig Babe
Paul Bakewich

Charles Barrett
Joan Biddell
Douglas Birkenshaw
Marie Black
Sheri Blake
Lorene Bourgeois
Alison Brooks
Tania Bortolotto
Tim Boyd
Chris Browne
Jay Carrol
Deborah Cheung
Dalibor Cizek
Greig Crysler
Michael Cumming
Zev Daniels
Martin Davidson
Wayne Deangelis
Carlos del Junco
Adrian Dicastri
Grant Diemart
Christopher Dunkley
Stuart Feldman
John Ferguson
Andrew Filarski
Matt Fisher
Anne Marie Fleming
Andrew Fox
Branka Gazibara
Shankar Gowri
Colin Graham
Chris Grant
Toby Greenbaum
Tony Griffin
Fred Handley
Courtenay Henry

Anneli Ronimois
Henze
Peter Heywood
David Hileman
Trevor Horne
Ahmed Imam
Jim Ireland
John Iwanski
Simon Jones
Rolf Kaartinen
Jadwiga
Kalinowska-Kowalik
George Kapelos
Jonathon King
Munying Kwun
Peter Legris
Alice Liang
Marilou Lobsinger
Jarle Lovlin
Gunta Mackars
Leah Maguire
Jana Makalik
Vicky Manica
Steve Mannell
Robert Marshall
Gary McCluskie
Michael McColl
Chris McCormack
Breck McFarlane
Sandra McKee
Sharon McKenzie
Barbara McLean
Sean McSweeny
Paul Mezei
Brenda Miller
Neil Morfitt

Joe Moro
Michael Morrissey
Rowley Mossop
Catherine Nasmith
Elie Newman
José Periera
Zenis Quesnel
Chris Radigan
Mario Rende
Avi Rosenberg
George Ross
Sandor Rott
Val Rynimeri
Ron Sandrin Litt
Paul Sapounzi
Kathryn Saunders
Frances Schmitt
Ari Shiff
Anne Sinclair
Jennifer Stanley
Mark Sterling
Christopher Stevens
Mike Szabo
Paul Szaszkiewicz
Peggy Theodore
Alan Vihant
Helen Vorster
Kit Wallace
Jane Warburton
David Weir
Tracy Winton
Leslie Woo
Michael Yuen
Marek Zawadzki

CONTRIBUTORS

ESMAIL BANIASSAD

Esmail Baniassad is a past president of the Royal Architectural Institute of Canada. He is a professor of architecture at the Technical University of Nova Scotia. He conceived and initiated the present series of monographs during his term as Dean of Faculty and is currently the general editor for TUNS Press.

BRIAN CARTER

Brian Carter is an architect who has worked in practice most recently with Arup Associates in London, and as a teacher in Europe and North America. A fellow of the Royal Society of Arts, he was recently appointed Professor and Chairman of Architecture at the University of Michigan.

ROBERT FULFORD

Robert Fulford, an arts journalist in Toronto for 35 years, writes a weekly column on cultural issues for The Globe and Mail and a column on architecture and planning for Toronto Life magazine. He edited Saturday Night magazine for 19 years. His most recent book is *Accidental City: The Transformation of Toronto.*

ACKNOWLEDGEMENTS

This Monograph, the second in the series of Canadian Documents in Architecture, has been prepared with the help and insight of a number of people. The continuing energetic support of Essy Baniassad – support which has provided clear advice, constructive criticism and critical readings of ideas, text and drawings – together with the encouragement of Frank Palermo through a continuing commitment of resources, have both been invaluable. Particular thanks must go to Jack Diamond and Donald Schmitt and to all their colleagues who have worked with them in the office in Toronto, for their time, persistent attention and the outstanding commitment to the creation of an architecture of substance. First and foremost, it is they who have designed the buildings which have been an inspiration – without that there would be little interest in having this publication. In making that commitment they have created of course the raw material for this publication and the drawings, descriptions and images which Steven Evans and Heather Lyons so energetically sought out, collated and made available. Steven Evans has also been responsible for taking many of the outstanding photographs which provide an important record and lasting impression of many of these buildings, whilst the writer Robert Fulford, through his thoughtful consideration, has revealed a range of other critical and original views of the work. The ever-reliable support of Donald Westin of TUNS Press in Halifax and the perceptive insights and detailed advice of Sunil Bhandari and Laurie Plater in Toronto were invaluable in realizing the design and production of this book.

Michael J. Hellyer, the Academic Affairs Officer of the Canadian High Commission in London, has continued to give encouragement to the publication of this series, as has the UK/Canada Architecture Group under the direction of its chairman Martin Birkhans from the University of Edinburgh. James E. Carter in Oxford provided inspiration and critical readings, and Grant Wanzel and Annette W. LeCuyer both very generously made space and time for me to work in Halifax, Greenwich and Ann Arbor. However it is the School of Architecture of the Technical University of Nova Scotia which deserves special acknowledgment for the continuing confidence and care they have given to developing the form and detail of this series of Documents in Canadian Architecture.

B.C.